YOU ARE ONE-THIRD **daffodil**

broadway books

NEW YORK

YOU

ARE ONE-THIRD
daffodil
AND OTHER FACTS TO AMAZE,
AMUSE, AND ASTOUND

Compiled by Tom Nuttall

Copyright © 2008, 2009 by Preface Publishing

All rights reserved.
Published in the United States by Broadway Books,
an imprint of the Crown Publishing Group,
a division of Random House, Inc., New York.
www.crownpublishing.com

BROADWAY BOOKS and the Broadway Books
colophon are trademarks of Random House, Inc.

Originally published in the United Kingdom as
In Fact by Preface Publishing, a division of the
Random House Group Ltd., London,
in 2008.

Library of Congress Cataloging-in-Publication Data
You are one-third daffodil: and other facts to
amaze, amuse, and astound / compiled by
Tom Nuttall.—1st U.S. ed.
     p.   cm.
   1. Handbooks, vade-mecums, etc. 2. Curiosities
and wonders. I. Nuttall, Tom. II. Title.
AG105.N94   2009
031.02—dc22   2009007687

ISBN 978-0-7679-3246-2

Printed in the United States

10 9 8 7 6 5 4 3 2 1

First U.S. Edition

For my former colleagues at *Prospect*—David Goodhart, fact filterer-in-chief; Susha-Lee Shothaman, whose fact radar is even more finely tuned than my own; and John Kelly, without whom this book would not have appeared

ACKNOWLEDGMENTS

Thanks first to my former colleagues at *Prospect*— this book is theirs as much as it is mine. David Goodhart invented the "In Fact" column and continues to act as fact filterer-in-chief. Susha Lee-Shothaman's fact radar is even more finely tuned than my own. And I salute the anonymous army of editorial assistants and interns whose labors kept "In Fact" going for six years before I arrived at *Prospect* and on whose factual shoulders I stood.

Without John Kelly, this book would not have appeared. Trevor Dolby at Preface in the UK got the project off the ground and has been helpful and encouraging throughout. Jenna Ciongoli and the team at Broadway provided gentle but masterful tweaks for the American edition.

Finally, it's a great pleasure to say that any factual errors in the book are *not* the responsibility of the author.

"Facts are stupid things," President Ronald Reagan told the Republican National Convention in 1988. And during the six years I compiled the "In Fact" column for *Prospect* magzine, I've occasionally felt the same. Yet for the most part we tend to revere facts; they drive scientific development, they fuel political debate, they fill up amusing books like this one. (Even Reagan was actually a fact fan. He had meant to tell his fellow Republicans that facts were stubborn things; it just came out wrong.)

A fact can, of course, be a slippery thing. Shorn of context, it can lend undeserved authority to a shoddy opinion; artfully combined with other carefully selected particulars, it can crowd out dissent. And despite our claims to the contrary, it's not always so clear that we do respect the things. Nine times out of ten, when someone writes in to *Prospect* accusing an article of getting its facts wrong, he or she actually turns out to be flustered not about the facts themselves, but about what the author has chosen to do with them.

"In Fact" traces its ancestry back to the very first issues of *Prospect*. The column was inspired by the famous "Index" from the monthly magazine *Harper's*, which presents a string of thematically connected facts, usually numerical, designed to cajole the reader into seeing the world the *Harper's* way. *Prospect*'s "In Fact," on the other hand, holds the facts themselves in esteem: their neutrality, their seriousness, sometimes their downright weirdness. "In Fact" is, admittedly, insulated from criticism by its device of attributing facts to third-party sources (the eagle-eyed reader may on occasion pause over the meaning of "*Prospect* research"). The magazine takes a "third-way" approach to the question of whether the facts themselves are "true," triangulating between old-fashioned objectivism and postmodern relativism. "In Fact" is, ironically, the only section of *Prospect* that isn't fact-checked; but at the same time, the magazine aims only to feature facts that have the whiff of truth about them. More important, the column, rather like *Prospect* itself, cleaves to no particular ideology and seeks only to publish the original, the provocative, and the stimulating (and, now and then, the crude).

If "In Fact" has ever aimed to do anything beyond

amuse and astound, it is perhaps to inspire its readers to see the world slightly differently. For instance, does the Israeli-Palestinian conflict not appear in a different light when you realize that the areas under dispute—the West Bank and the Gaza Strip—are roughly the same size as, respectively, Delaware and Detroit? Or what about the strange shock to one's sense of historical chronology that comes from learning that Galileo was offered an academic seat at Harvard (he turned it down)?

Prospect readers often told me that "In Fact" was the part of the magazine they turned to first each month. In my early days at *Prospect,* as an editorial assistant with little influence over the rest of the magazine, I got a real kick out of comments like this. I was even known to exclaim that "In Fact" represented the "essence" of *Prospect*; after all, didn't articles sometimes get edited down to short diary items, and didn't diary items sometimes get compressed into single facts? Still, this hubris didn't prepare me for what happened one day in January 2003. We were wrapping up the latest issue of *Prospect*; it was one in the morning, the magazine had to go to the printer that night, and, as usual, I was floundering around for facts to fill the column. Desperate to allow my superiors to get to bed, I turned to the fact source of last resort: Google. An unimaginative search for "interesting facts" led me to the personal website of an undergraduate student. And there, nestling like a pearl among photos of boozy nights out and lists of favorite bands, I saw it: "Most toilets flush in E-flat." Perfect. Alas, *Prospect*'s high standards for sources meant I wouldn't be able to credit my savior (and I hadn't invented "*Prospect* research" yet), and so I was forced to seek out a mainstream alternative; Google helpfully led me to the slightly sinister-sounding Centers for Disease Control and Prevention. Job done.

The issue was published a few days later. I was enjoying a well-deserved morning of sleeping in when I was woken by the squeal of my mobile phone. I answered blearily and found myself in conversation with an excitable producer from the UK TV chat show *Johnny Vaughan Tonight*, who wanted to know everything about the toilet fact: Where did I get it from? Was it really true? Had I verified it? I patiently directed her to the CDC website and went back to sleep, pleased to have discovered that the long arms of "In Fact" stretched as far as prime-time television.

Later that day, idly flicking through *The Guardian*, I was brought up short by the paper's third leading article. Entitled "Closet Composers," it was an elegant meditation on the question of whether the fact that toilets flush in E-flat, as revealed in *Prospect*, could shed new light on the provenance of some of history's musical masterpieces. (The paper noted Wagner's claim that the opening passage of the Ring cycle, a sustained

E-flat in the double basses, was inspired by a dream in which he had heard the sound of "swiftly running water.")

Already buoyed by the day's brace of triumphs, I made it a hat trick in the evening when *Mark Lawson's Front Row,* a radio arts show, decided to send a musicologist armed with a tuning fork into the toilets of the BBC's Broadcasting House to test the veracity of the claim. (I wasn't exactly surprised when it turned out to be hokum.) So there you go: the power of one fact—or "fact"—to set the day's news agenda. And from there the fact snowballed into the collective consciousness; even now I occasionally come across it in surprising places. A couple of years ago, the radio station Classic FM made use of it in an advertising campaign, and apparently it even made it on to the *Late Show with David Letterman.*

My fact antennae soon became finely honed; the era of late-night fact scrambles passed quickly. I became so tuned in to the facts around me that while I was editing the fact selection for this book, I sometimes found myself thinking, "How interesting, must remember that for the column." Such assiduousness could bear fruit: I might be having a chat in the pub, for instance, and someone would say, "Did you know . . ."—instantly I would be on fact alert. If the claim was interesting and could be corroborated, it was in. And after years of this sort of thing, some of my friends decided they wanted a piece of the fun and so they acted as my fact scouts—plenty of the facts in this book owe their appearance to such diligence.

Hope you enjoy this collection.

Tom Nuttall

YOU ARE ONE-THIRD daffodil

Coming into This World . . .

Facts About Birth and Babies

At birth, most babies cry at C or C-sharp.

—*FINANCIAL TIMES*, JULY 31, 2003

At a rough estimate, each newly conceived human has around three hundred harmful genetic mutations.

—EDGE.ORG

The "happiness boost" that men gain from a first-born son is 75 percent larger than from a firstborn daughter. Second and third children don't contribute to the happiness of either parent.

—*PSYCHOLOGY TODAY*, APRIL 12, 2007

Every day, 44,000 babies are born in China—
roughly the population of Canterbury.

—PROSPECT RESEARCH

Most babies in Britain are conceived without the con-
scious consent of the father.

—INSTITUTE FOR PUBLIC POLICY RESEARCH

Sixty percent of newborn babies in India would be in
intensive care if born in California.

—STATE OF THE WORLD 2000

A boy born in Russia in 2004 had a lower life expectancy than one born in Bangladesh.

—THE NEW YORKER, OCTOBER 11, 2004

In 2006, for the first time, more French children
were born out of wedlock than to married parents.

—REUTERS, JANUARY 15, 2008

Hong Kong's fertility rate—1.02 children per woman—is the second lowest in the world. The rate in Macau is 0.91

— *CIA WORLD FACTBOOK*

In Berlin, 20 percent more babies were born in March 2007—nine months after the World Cup—than in March 2006. — *FINANCIAL TIMES,* JUNE 9, 2007

American women are 70 percent more likely to die in childbirth than Europeans.

— *TIMES LITERARY SUPPLEMENT,* JUNE 1, 2007

Almost 1 percent of Guatemalan children are adopted by American families.

— *THE NEW YORK TIMES,* NOVEMBER 6, 2006

Eighty-six percent of fathers attend the birth of their children. —FATHERHOOD INSTITUTE

The fertility rate in the United States—2.1 children per woman—is the highest it has been for thirty-five years. — *THE NEW YORK TIMES*, FEBRUARY 1, 2008

❓

In 2000, for the first time in more than two hundred years, more babies were born in France than in any other European country.

— *OLD EUROPE? DEMOGRAPHIC CHANGE AND PENSION REFORM* BY DAVID WILLETTS, CENTER FOR EUROPEAN REFORM

❗

New Zealand and Britain are two of the few countries in which a majority of married couples practicing family planning opt for male rather than female sterilization. —EARTH POLICY INSTITUTE

❓

Forty-three percent of Americans approve of using gene therapy to enhance the physical and behavioral traits of children.

—THE PEW RESEARCH CENTER FOR THE PEOPLE & THE PRESS

❗

By the age of fifteen, only half of American children live with both biological parents, compared with roughly two-thirds of Swedish, German, and French children and 90 percent of children in Spain and Italy. — *THE AMERICAN PROSPECT,* JUNE 2005

. . . And Leaving It

Facts About Death and Dying

Five people were killed by falling icicles in the central Russian town of Samara between February 23 and 25, 2008.   —REUTERS, FEBRUARY 26, 2008

The Scottish suicide rate is almost double that of England: 21 per 100,000 people compared with 12 per 100,000.   —*FINANCIAL TIMES*, JANUARY 16, 2004

The life expectancy of professional cyclists is about fifty.   —*THE NEW CRITERION*, JUNE 2004

There are 87.4 violent deaths per 100,000 people in Lithuania: the highest figure in the world.

—WORLD HEALTH ORGANIZATION

Bird flu kills someone almost every week in Indonesia.   —THE ASSOCIATED PRESS, APRIL 24, 2007

Venezuela has the highest per capita murder rate in the world.   —*FOREIGN POLICY*, MAY/JUNE 2007

Americans have a 1 in 180 chance of dying from poisoning. The odds of dying in a car accident are 247 to 1, of drowning in the bath 9,377 to 1, and of being burned to death by ignited nightwear 538,523 to 1.   —ECONOMIST.COM, SEPTEMBER 8, 2008

Between 20 and 50 percent of deaths from hypothermia involve "paradoxical undressing" (the sufferer removing their own clothes).

—*NEW SCIENTIST*, APRIL 21, 2007

Between 25,000 and 100,000 Indian farmers commit
suicide every year. — *THE HINDU*, FEBRUARY 25, 2007

Suicide is the biggest killer among young Chinese.
It also accounts for a third of all deaths among rural
women. —MARGINAL REVOLUTION, JUNE 30, 2006

Every year 1.2 million people die in road accidents
around the world. — *THE OBSERVER*, MARCH 23, 2008

In the United States, more than 90 percent of suicide
attempts involving guns are successful. The success
rate for jumping from high places is 34 percent, and
for drug overdoses just 2 percent.

— *TIME*, JUNE 30, 2008

In the United States, on the third and fourth days
after heavyweight championship bouts, the homicide rate rises by an average of 9 percent.

— *HAPPINESS* BY RICHARD LAYARD

Between 1948 and 1998, 20,362 Israelis were killed in wars with neighboring states while 20,852 were killed on the roads.

— *THE JERUSALEM REPORT,* NOVEMBER 22, 1999

More people die as a result of dog attacks in the United States each year than have been killed by sharks in the last hundred years.

— *THE SUNDAY TELEGRAPH,* AUGUST 5, 2007

Between 1969 and 2002, a citizen of Northern Ireland was over two hundred times more likely to die from sectarian violence than a citizen of India.

— *PROSPECT,* MAY 2002

In the United States in the twentieth century, five times more people were killed in traffic accidents than died in war. Total fatalities on the road as of 1997 were 2.98 million, compared with war deaths totaling 605,000. — *PROSPECT* RESEARCH

Seventy-one percent of dead bodies in Britain are cremated, but in Ireland the figure is only 5 percent.

—PROSPECT, APRIL 2003

A 2005 survey in Sweden found that for every two inches in height, men's suicide rate decreased by 9 percent. But a more recent study has found an even stronger correlation between male body length at birth and the probability of an attempt at suicide in later life.

—THE WILSON QUARTERLY, SPRING 2008

The three most common requests by British people planning their own funerals are to be cremated with their pet's ashes, to have a mobile phone in the coffin, and for someone to ensure that they are dead.

—AGE CONCERN

The average American lives thirteen years longer than the average celebrity, who is four times as likely to commit suicide.

—TIME.COM

It is forbidden to die in the Norwegian town of
Longyearbyen.
—BBC RADIO 4, JULY 12, 2008

Fifty-six percent of the world's female suicides are in
China.
—*CHINA SHAKES THE WORLD*, BY JAMES KYNGE

An estimated 7,000 Americans a year die as a result
of doctors' bad handwriting.
—*HARPER'S*, APRIL 2007

You Say Potato, I Say Potato

Facts About Languages and Words

On a QWERTY keyboard, 32 percent of keystrokes take place on the "home" (middle) row, 52 percent on the upper row, and 16 percent on the bottom row.

—JARED DIAMOND, *DISCOVER* MAGAZINE, APRIL 1997

Egyptians, Indians, and Turks search for "sex" on Google more than any other nationality. "Hitler" is most popular in Germany, Austria, and Mexico; "Nazi" in Chile, Australia, and Britain. "David Beckham" gets the most hits in Venezuela.

—REUTERS, OCTOBER 17, 2007

The insults "moron," "idiot," "imbecile," and "cretin" were all once official medical diagnoses.

— BALDERDASH & PIFFLE, BBC 2

"Stewardesses" is the longest word typed with only the left hand and "lollipop" with the right.

— URBANDICTIONARY.COM

Counting up from zero, and excluding the word "and," the first number to contain the letter A is one thousand.

— PROSPECT RESEARCH

In the Eskimo language Inuktitut, there is a single word meaning "I should try not to become an alcoholic": *Iminngernaveersaartunngortussaavunga.*

— THE NEW YORK SUN, DECEMBER 28, 2006

The words "tomato," "coyote," "avocado," and "chocolate" all come from the Aztec language Nahuatl.

— MARGINAL REVOLUTION, FEBRUARY 27, 2006

The highest possible legal score on a first turn in Scrabble is given by the word "muzjiks," giving 128 points. The world record for the highest score on a single turn is "quixotry" (365 points).

—WIKIPEDIA/SLATE, OCTOBER 26, 2006

The collective noun for owls is "parliament."

—WIKIPEDIA

No words in the English language rhyme with "orange," "silver," "purple," or "month."

—NEW SCIENTIST, DECEMBER 18, 2004

The word "boredom" did not exist in the English language until after 1750.

—BOREDOM: THE LITERARY HISTORY OF A STATE OF MIND
BY PATRICIA M. SPACKS

There is no word for "please" in Gujarati.

—NEW STATESMAN, JULY 25, 2005

Because Chinese number words are so brief, the average Chinese speaker can hold nine digits in his or her active memory at once, compared to seven for English speakers.　—*THE NEW YORKER*, MARCH 3, 2008

There are 500,000 words in *The Oxford English Dictionary*. French has less than a fifth of this number.

—*THE DAY BRITAIN DIED* BY ANDREW MARR

"Queueing" is the only word in English with five consecutive vowels.　—*PROSPECT* RESEARCH

The word "paradise" comes from a Persian word meaning "walled around."

—*FENCING PARADISE* BY RICHARD MABEY

The "zip" in "zip code" stands for "zone improvement plan."　—*CHICAGO TRIBUNE*, DECEMBER 2, 2002

An eighteen-year-old knows 60,000 words, which represents a learning rate of one word per ninety waking minutes from the age of one.

— THE LANGUAGE INSTINCT BY STEVEN PINKER

There are 823 languages spoken in Papua New Guinea, more than any other country in the world.

— LIMITS OF LANGUAGE BY MIKAEL PARKVALL

"Broadcast" is a term borrowed from farmers, describing what they do with seeds across a field.

— THE WEEKLY STANDARD, JUNE 14, 2004

By the age of five, children have acquired 85 percent of the language they will have as adults.

—JOHN BASTIANI, RSA LECTURE

The first written Afrikaans used Arabic script, rather than Roman.

— PROSPECT, MAY 2004

Of all the words in *The Oxford English Dictionary*, 99 percent derive from languages other than Old English. However, words that derive from Old English make up 62 percent of the words most used.

—*THE POWER OF BABEL* BY JOHN MCWHORTER

The Finnish language has no future tense.

—WIKIPEDIA

There are no plurals in Chinese.

—*WIRED*, DECEMBER 2006

The five most-used nouns in the English language are "time," "person," "year," "way," and "day."

—CNN, JUNE 22, 2006

The fourteenth most popular search term entered into Google is "Google."   —*TIME*, JUNE 6, 2007

The term "blockbuster" was coined in the 1920s, referring to a film whose queue of customers at the box office was so long that it could not be contained on a single city block.

— *THE WASHINGTON POST,* FEBRUARY 27, 2005

Jack Kerouac typed at one hundred words a minute.

— *THE NEW YORKER,* APRIL 9, 2007

Over just six days in August 1998, *The Washington Post* devoted 80,289 words to the Monica Lewinsky scandal.

— *THE NEW REPUBLIC,* SEPTEMBER 7, 1998

The condition of being unable to release a dart from one's hand when throwing is known as dartitis.

— *PROSPECT* RESEARCH

Into the Wild

Facts About Animals

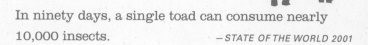

In ninety days, a single toad can consume nearly
10,000 insects. —STATE OF THE WORLD 2001

An amputated newt limb will grow back fully within
ten weeks.

—THE CHRONICLE OF HIGHER EDUCATION, JANUARY 31, 2003

The fruit fly *Drosophila bifurca* is 1.5 millimeters
long, while its sperm are 6 centimeters long.

—NATURE, JULY 6, 2000

A cow burps up to 280 liters of methane per day.

— THE GUARDIAN, JUNE 7, 2001

Seven percent of male zebra finches stutter.

— THE OBSERVER, FEBRUARY 24, 2008

The average bee produces one-twelfth of a teaspoon of honey during its lifetime.   *— HORIZONS*, MARCH 2003

Butterflies taste with their feet.

— TORONTO STAR, MAY 28, 2002

Garden worms have five pairs of hearts.

—CORNELL UNIVERSITY

Research on guinea pigs has resulted in twenty-three Nobel prizes.

—A GUINEA PIG'S HISTORY OF BIOLOGY BY JIM ENDERSBY

The penis of a barnacle may reach up to twenty
times its body size. — *THE INDEPENDENT,* AUGUST 27, 2004

Rats can run a hundred yards in less than ten seconds and can jump six feet in the air.

— *DAILY MIRROR,* AUGUST 23, 2003

Neither rabbits nor mice can vomit.

— NATIONAL ANTI-VIVISECTION SOCIETY

A female ferret will die if it goes into heat and cannot find a mate. — FERRETSMAGAZINE.COM

The closest living relative of the *Tyrannosaurus rex*
is the chicken. — *THE GUARDIAN,* APRIL 13, 2007

Half of all animal species are parasites.

Bacteria of the species *Pseudomonas fluorescens* can grow from a population of five hundred to two hundred million over the course of one night.

Ants spend only one-fifth of their day working.

Only 3 percent of male birds have a penis.

Adult "paradoxical frogs," which are found in the Amazon and Trinidad, are so named because they are a third of the size of their tadpoles.

The Exxon *Valdez* oil spill in 1989 killed 250,000 birds. This is approximately the same number that die colliding with plate glass every day in the United States.
— *PROSPECT*, OCTOBER 2001

?

At any moment, there are almost twice as many chickens alive as humans.
— *PLANET CHICKEN* BY HATTIE ELLIS

!

There are twice as many privately owned tigers in America as there are in the wild across the world.
— *THE GUARDIAN*, FEBRUARY 2, 2007

?

Homosexual behavior occurs in more than 450 different kinds of animals.
— *BIOLOGICAL EXUBERANCE* BY BRUCE BAGEMIHL

!

In Japan, dogs now outnumber children age ten and under—there were 13.1 million dogs in 2006.
— ABC NEWS, AUGUST 28, 2007

In 2001, the year of the foot-and-mouth epidemic in the U.K., fewer animals were culled or slaughtered than in an average year.

—DAVID KING, FORMER CHIEF SCIENTIFIC ADVISER
TO THE BRITISH GOVERNMENT

Elephants cannot jump.   —*DAILY MAIL*, JANUARY 24, 2008

They Did What?!

Facts About Some

Illustrious Individuals

Hitler was on the short list for the 1938 Nobel Peace Prize. —*THE GUARDIAN*, DECEMBER 7, 2002

Vladimir Nabokov spent seven years as a research fellow in entomology at Harvard.

—*AT LARGE AND AT SMALL: CONFESSIONS OF A LITERARY HEDONIST* BY ANNE FADIMAN

In the 1930s, the Inland Revenue investigated William Butler Yeats's tax returns because they could not believe a poet of his stature had sales that were so small. —*THE GUARDIAN*, OCTOBER 13, 2005

Portuguese soccer star Cristiano Ronaldo was
named after Ronald Reagan.

—UEFA EURO 2004 WEBSITE

Woodrow Wilson is the only president to have had a
PhD.

—WOODROW WILSON INTERNATIONAL CENTER FOR SCHOLARS

Casanova spent the last thirteen years of his life
working as a librarian.

— *THE SUNDAY TIMES MAGAZINE,* APRIL 23, 2005

The only two people to have won both a Nobel Prize
and an Oscar are George Bernard Shaw and Al Gore.

— *THE INDEPENDENT,* OCTOBER 13, 2007

Aldous Huxley died on the same day John F. Kennedy
was assassinated.

— *THE NEW YORKER,* JUNE 26, 2006

Einstein did not learn to read until he was ten.

— *THE GUARDIAN*, DECEMBER 6, 2001

Napoleon was actually five feet six and a half, taller than the average early nineteenth-century Frenchman.

— *THE OBSERVER*, MARCH 25, 2007

Donald Rumsfeld, who served in both the Nixon and George W. Bush cabinets, is both the youngest and the oldest defense secretary in U.S. history.

—BBC.CO.UK, DECEMBER 28, 2006

Bill Gates gets 4 million emails a day.

— *NEW STATESMAN*, JANUARY 25, 2007

Science fiction writer Ray Bradbury avoids computers and ATMs and claims never to have driven a car. Isaac Asimov refused to board an airplane.

— *DISCOVER*, JANUARY 30, 2008

In 1996, Mahathir Mohamad, prime minister of Malaysia, threw the largest-ever dinner party. Twelve thousand guests celebrated the fiftieth anniversary of Mahathir's ruling party, the United Malays National Organization.

—BBC WORLD SERVICE

❶

The FBI had a 1,427-page dossier on Albert Einstein.

—*FORWARD*, JUNE 14, 2002

❷

The musician Moby (real name Richard Melville Hall) is the great-great-grand-nephew of Herman Melville, author of *Moby-Dick*. Moby was a childhood nickname.

—SUCCESSWHOSMYDADDY.COM

❶

Andrew Jackson personally fought in 103 duels.

—*WASHINGTON MONTHLY*, MARCH 2007

❷

When Fidel Castro took power in Cuba, he ordered all Monopoly sets to be destroyed.

—HASBRO

Catherine de Medici introduced knickers in France in the sixteenth century, as she preferred to ride horses sidesaddle. — *THE SUNDAY TIMES*, OCTOBER 23, 2005

Ronald Reagan was born six years before John F. Kennedy. — *PROSPECT* RESEARCH

Lauren Bacall and Shimon Peres are first cousins. — *JEWISH BULLETIN*, MAY 16, 2003

The IRS has a computer devoted solely to Bill Gates's tax return. — *THE GUARDIAN*, FEBRUARY 11, 2006

Walt Disney was a direct 22nd-generation descendant of King Edward I.

— *ON ROYALTY* BY JEREMY PAXMAN

Paul Wolfowitz, formerly deputy defense secretary and head of the World Bank, speaks French, German, Arabic, Hebrew, and Indonesian.

— THE NEW YORKER, APRIL 9, 2007

Albert Einstein is the fifth highest-earning dead celebrity, "earning" $18 million in 2006 from use of his trademarked name on the Disney-owned "Baby Einstein" brand of videos and toys. Royalties go to Jerusalem's Hebrew University, which was bequeathed the estate.

— FORBES.COM, OCTOBER 29, 2007

Between thirty and forty-five paparazzi follow Britney Spears around on an average evening.

— THE ATLANTIC, APRIL 2008

In 2006, the richest person in mainland China was Zhang Yin, a paper recycling entrepreneur worth $3.4 billion. Zhang, the world's richest self-made woman, is one of fifteen billionaires in China.

— FINANCIAL TIMES, OCTOBER 10, 2006

After Marilyn Monroe's death in 1962, the suicide rate in the United States temporarily increased by 12 percent. — *THE TIPPING POINT* BY MALCOLM GLADWELL

One of Olivia Newton-John's grandfathers was Max Born, a Nobel-winning physicist and one of the founders of quantum mechanics.

— THE DAILY DISH, NOVEMBER 6, 2006

Charlie Chaplin once entered a Charlie Chaplin look-alike contest—and failed to make the finals.

— SNOPES.COM

Nelson Mandela was not removed from the U.S. terror watch list until 2008.

— *THE DAILY TELEGRAPH*, JULY 2, 2008

Elvis Presley's manager, Colonel Tom Parker, stopped
Elvis from touring abroad, as Parker was an illegal
immigrant and believed he would not be allowed
back into the United States.   —BBC.CO.UK

Come Rain or Shine

Facts About the Weather

Two-thirds of the world's people have never seen snow. — *CANADIAN WEATHER TRIVIA CALENDAR 2008*

In New York City, January 2008 was the first essentially snowless January in seventy-five years.

—LIVESCIENCE.COM, JANUARY 30, 2008

Per capita, Sudan has more rainfall than Britain.

— *THE DAILY TELEGRAPH,* MARCH 2, 2006

At any given moment, there are about 1,800 thunderstorms happening around the world. Approximately one hundred lightning bolts strike the Earth every second. —WEATHERMETRICS.COM

From a height of three kilometers, it takes thirty minutes for a snowflake to reach the ground.
— *CANADIAN WEATHER TRIVIA CALENDAR 2008*

When rainfall is significantly below normal, the risk of low-level conflict escalating to full-scale civil war approximately doubles in the following year.
— *NEW SCIENTIST,* JUNE 2, 2007

Each year, 30,000 to 80,000 meteorites land on Earth. —NATURAL HISTORY MUSEUM, LONDON

It rains twice as much in Sydney as in London.
— *THE GUARDIAN,* NOVEMBER 8, 2004

On average, London's commuters get wet just twelve
times a year. — TRANSPORT FOR LONDON

Between 8 and 15 percent of the increase in American life expectancy over the last thirty years is the
result of people moving to warmer climates.

— *THE NEW YORK TIMES*, JANUARY 12, 2008

Battle of the Sexes

Facts About Men and Women

The average British woman spends two years of her life gazing in the mirror.   — *THE TIMES,* FEBRUARY 7, 2007

Forty-four percent of PhDs in biology and the life sciences are awarded to women.   —EDGE.ORG

The Wimbledon women's finalists in 2001—Venus Williams (6'1″) and Lindsay Davenport (6'2½″)—had a greater combined height than the men's finalists.

— *PROSPECT* RESEARCH

Women spend nearly three years of their lives getting ready to leave the house. Men spend three months waiting for their wives and girlfriends while out shopping. —*DAILY MAIL*, NOVEMBER 25, 2007

A typical man is 50 to 70 percent water, a typical woman, 40 to 60 percent.

—*ROCKY MOUNTAIN NEWS*, APRIL 15, 2003

On average, women take three times as long to use the toilet as men. —BRITISH TOILET ASSOCIATION

Men produce twice as much saliva as women.

—*PSYCHOLOGY TODAY*, JULY/AUGUST 2003

Men and women differ genetically by 1 to 2 percent—as wide a gap as the one that separates women from female chimpanzees.

—*THE BOSTON GLOBE*, JULY 6, 2003

Seventy-four percent of the women passengers aboard the *Titanic* survived, compared with 20 percent of the men. — *THE WEEKLY STANDARD,* APRIL 10, 2006

In March 2009 Monaco became the last country to appoint a female member of government.

— WORLDWIDE GUIDE TO WOMEN IN LEADERSHIP

Women earn 57 percent of bachelor's degrees and 59 percent of master's degrees in the United States, and a majority of research PhDs, but only 24 percent of PhDs in the physical sciences.

— THE SURVEY OF EARNED DOCTORATES

In the United States, twelve percent of women with MBAs are divorced or separated, compared with 5 percent of men with MBAs.

— *THE WALL STREET JOURNAL,* APRIL 1, 2008

YOU ARE ONE-THIRD **daffodil**

In Chicago and New York, among other American cities, full-time female employees in their twenties earn more on average than males.

—QUEENS COLLEGE, NEW YORK

In Brazil, 62 percent of higher education students are women. —BRAZILIAN MINISTRY OF EDUCATION

Eighty percent of British fathers think of Christmas as a "relaxing holiday break"; only 35 percent of mothers share this view.

—*HAVING NONE OF IT* BY SUZANNE FRANKS

In 2006, more women (244) than men (234) were ordained as clergy in the Church of England for the first time since the introduction of women priests in 1994. —*THE GUARDIAN*, NOVEMBER 14, 2007

French males cannot marry until they are eighteen, but females can marry at only fifteen.

—*THE GUARDIAN*, MARCH 30, 2005

In the United States in 2005, one-third of wives out-earned their husbands.

— *THE WALL STREET JOURNAL,* APRIL 1, 2008

Half the men in the United States say they feel nervous in the company of women.

— *CONVERSATION* BY THEODORE ZELDIN

Women make up 70 percent of Algeria's lawyers and 60 percent of its judges.

— *THE NEW YORK TIMES,* MAY 26, 2007

Women drivers are three times more likely than men to suffer whiplash injuries if their car is hit from behind, because they generally sit closer to the steering wheel.

—BBC

DON'T FORGET TO FLUSH!

Facts About the Thing We Use Every Day

Most toilets flush in E-flat.

—CENTERS FOR DISEASE CONTROL AND PREVENTION

¡?!

One American in 6,500 is injured by a toilet seat during their lifetime.

—*THE PARANOID'S POCKET GUIDE* BY CAMERON TUTTLE

¡?!

Wembley Stadium in London has 2,600 toilets—more than any building in the world.

—*EVENING STANDARD,* MAY 1, 2007

Planes, Trains, and Automobiles

Facts About How We Get Around

Africa has less than 4 percent of the world's air traffic, but one-third of its air disasters. Around two-thirds of the airlines banned by the European Union on safety grounds are African. —*MONOCLE*, MAY 2007

In 2002, more people in India traveled by train in one day than by plane in the entire year.

—SHASHI THAROOR

Since 1970, global bicycle production has nearly quadrupled while car production has doubled.

—ECONOMIST.COM, SEPTEMBER 22, 2008

Seventy percent of Land Rovers—first built in
1948—are still on the road.   — *TOP GEAR*

While fifty to two hundred "large" pieces of man-
made space debris return to Earth every year, ex-
perts know of only one report of a person being hit.
Lottie Williams of Tulsa, Oklahoma, was struck on
the shoulder in 1997 by a small piece of debris from
a discarded piece of a Delta rocket. She was unhurt.

—THE ASSOCIATED PRESS, FEBRUARY 20, 2008

The civil aviation industry estimates that eight thousand bags are misrouted on the world's airways
every day.

— *AVIATION TERRORISM AND SECURITY*, EDITED BY
PAUL WILKINSON AND BRIAN M. JENKINS

Europe's merchant ships emit around a third more
carbon than aircraft do.

— *THE ECONOMIST*, JUNE 10, 2006

Half the world's supertankers are disassembled at Chittagong port in Bangladesh.

—FOREIGN POLICY, JANUARY/FEBRUARY 2006

❶

In 2006, there were seventy-seven major commercial plane crashes worldwide, the lowest number ever recorded. Only twenty involved fatalities.

—FOREIGN POLICY, NOVEMBER/DECEMBER 2007

❷

In Britain, five times as much money is taken from motorists in taxes as is spent on transport. In the United States, the figures are equal.

—BBC.CO.UK

❶

In 2001, there was not a single traffic light in the Palestinian territories.

—THE NEW YORK REVIEW OF BOOKS, JUNE 22, 2006

❷

In Denmark, people buying a new car must pay a registration fee of approximately 105 percent of the car's value.

—THE WALL STREET JOURNAL, APRIL 16, 2007

India has just 1 percent of the world's vehicles but about 10 percent of annual road fatalities.

—*FINANCIAL TIMES*, APRIL 10, 2007

Soviet-made airplanes once made up 26 percent of the world's aircraft fleet.

—*THE WALL STREET JOURNAL*, DECEMBER 20, 2002

Dallas/Fort Worth International Airport is larger than Manhattan.

—*THE GLOBAL SOUL* BY PICO IYER

On average, British Airways loses nine sets of luggage for every jumbo flight.

—*THE GUARDIAN*, FEBRUARY 23, 2008

Over 90 percent of airplane crashes have survivors.

—BBC.CO.UK, OCTOBER 3, 2006

Sixty percent of all Porsches ever built are still on
the road.   —PORSCHE

❶

Ladders are dropped on Los Angeles freeways more
than any other item.   — *TRAFFIC* BY TOM VANDERBILT

❷

China owns no aircraft carriers.
                              —REAL CLEAR POLITICS, MAY 28, 2007

❶

When the Channel Tunnel opened in 1994, 15.9 million annual Eurostar passengers were forecast. The
actual number was 18 percent of that: 2.9 million. In
2001, passenger numbers were 6.9 million.
                        — *MEGAPROJECTS AND RISK* BY BENT FLYVBJERG

❷

The Irish drive an average 15,000 miles a year, more
than Americans and the British.
                              — *THE WEEK*, DECEMBER 31, 2004

❶

More than half of the London Underground network
is aboveground.   — *PROSPECT* RESEARCH

The Atlanta airport is the world's busiest.

— *THE ECONOMIST*, AUGUST 30, 2008

In 2007, twenty-four people killed themselves by
jumping under Paris Métro trains. On the New York
City Subway the figure was twenty-six, and on the
London Underground fifty.   — *TIME*, JULY 29, 2008

Americans collectively drove 11 billion fewer miles
in March 2008 than in March 2007.

—U.S. DEPARTMENT OF TRANSPORTATION

International Affairs

Facts About Countries Around the World

Every year, an average of twelve Japanese tourists in Paris have to be repatriated due to severe culture shock. —FOREIGN POLICY PASSPORT, DECEMBER 23, 2006

❶

There are 731 crimes in Glasgow for every 100,000 people, compared to 631 in New York City.
—REFORM SCOTLAND REPORT, "POWER FOR THE PUBLIC"

❷

Before a recent expansion, the Qatari national anthem lasted thirty-two seconds. The Greek national anthem has 158 verses. —NATIONAL-ANTHEMS.ORG

In the United States, 14.5 percent of men are six feet or over. But among CEOs of Fortune 500 companies, the figure is 58 percent.

— *BLINK* BY MALCOLM GLADWELL

The five most philanthropic American states, relative to their own wealth, are Mississippi, Arkansas, Oklahoma, Louisiana, and Alabama.

—CATALOGUEFORPHILANTHROPY.ORG

In two countries—Ivory Coast and Ghana—the proportion of people who say they have a "favorable opinion" of the United States is higher than in the United States itself.

—PEW RESEARCH CENTER FOR THE PEOPLE & THE PRESS

In 2004, the average European man overtook the average American man in height for the first time since 1775.

—BBC.CO.UK, APRIL 14, 2004

There are more burglaries per head in Canada than in the United States.

— *THE ECONOMIST*, OCTOBER 1, 2005

The Valley of Peace cemetery in Najaf, Iraq, is the biggest in the world, covering five square miles and containing over 5 million graves.

— *PROSPECT*, NOVEMBER 2004

Since 1945, average height in Japan has increased by nearly five inches.

— *TIMES LITERARY SUPPLEMENT*, FEBRUARY 25, 2005

Mozambique's flag features a Kalashnikov—the only gun to appear on a national flag.

— *THE GUN THAT CHANGED THE WORLD* BY MIKHAIL KALASHNIKOV

Romania has had six different national anthems since the Second World War.

— *THE WALL STREET JOURNAL*, MAY 17, 2002

Israelis own 10 percent of the private land on the
moon.   —*THE JERUSALEM POST,* JANUARY 4, 2007

No Chinese national has ever won a Nobel Prize.
                                          —*PROSPECT* RESEARCH

In Japan, there is one vending machine for every
twenty-three people.
          —JAPAN VENDING MACHINE MANUFACTURERS ASSOCIATION

The average Dutchman is six foot one, around four
inches taller than the average British or American
man.   —MSNBC, July 22, 2006

In 2003, American companies invested twice as
much in Ireland as they did in China.
                    —*FOREIGN POLICY,* SEPTEMBER/OCTOBER 2005

America's prison population is higher than China's.

—CROOKED TIMBER

The U.S. Navy is as large as the next seventeen navies in the world combined.

—*INTERNATIONAL HERALD TRIBUNE*, AUGUST 8, 2007

Over one-fifth of the members of Pakistan's parliament are women—compared to 17 percent of members of the U.S. Congress.

—INTER-PARLIAMENTARY UNION

Canada supplies the United States with more oil than all the Persian Gulf nations put together.

—*THE NEW YORKER*, NOVEMBER 12, 2007

Per capita, there are more psychoanalysts in Buenos Aires than anywhere in the world.

—*THE DAILY TELEGRAPH*, JANUARY 14, 2006

The three most corrupt states, measured by convictions, are Alaska, Mississippi, and Louisiana. The least corrupt are Colorado, Wisconsin, and Nebraska.   — *GLOBAL CORRUPTION REPORT 2005*

Britons buy almost half as many celebrity magazines as Americans, despite a population only one-fifth the size.   — *THE ECONOMIST,* SEPTEMBER 3, 2005

Each year Ireland generates 869 kilograms of waste per head, 25 percent more than Denmark, its nearest European Union rival.

— *THE ECONOMIST,* SEPTEMBER 2, 2006

In 2006, the Swedish town of Södertälje took in twice as many Iraqi refugees as the entire United States.   — *THE NEW YORK TIMES,* JUNE 13, 2007

In Paraguay, dueling is legal if both participants are registered blood donors.

— *THE GUARDIAN* WORLD CUP 2006 GUIDE

The United States—with 5 percent of the world's population—houses 25 percent of the world's prison inmates. Its incarceration rate (714 per 100,000 residents) is almost 40 percent greater than those of its nearest competitors (the Bahamas, Belarus, and Russia).

— *BOSTON REVIEW*, JULY/AUGUST 2007

Twenty percent of all luxury goods are sold in Japan, and another 30 percent to Japanese traveling abroad—meaning Japanese buy half of all luxury goods in the world.

— *DELUXE: HOW LUXURY LOST ITS LUSTER* BY DANA THOMAS

Turkey granted the vote to women before France, Italy, Switzerland, or Belgium.

— *FINANCIAL TIMES*, OCTOBER 3, 2005

Per capita, Australia emits 30 percent more green-house gases than the United States.

—ADAM SMITH INSTITUTE

Ethiopia's calendar is more than seven years behind that of the rest of the world. The country held its millennium celebrations in 2007.

—BBC NEWS

When average disposable income is adjusted for the cost of living, Scandinavians are the poorest people in western Europe; the Spanish and the Portuguese are the richest.

—KPMG

In Milan, it is a legal requirement to smile at all times, except during funerals or hospital visits.

—LAW SOCIETY

Per capita, more people are diagnosed with skin can-cer each week in Scotland than in Australia.

—*THE GUARDIAN*, FEBRUARY 24, 2006

In the heyday of protectionism in South Korea, people violating foreign-currency regulations were subject to the death penalty.

— BOOKFORUM, FEBRUARY/MARCH 2008

In Sweden, prison sentences of more than five years are given out only for serious crimes like drug dealing, murder, and rape. In 2004, just 329 people were serving such sentences.

— THE NEW YORK TIMES MAGAZINE, FEBRUARY 5, 2006

The French consume more tranquilizers per head than any other nation.   — GEORGES CALVET

In Japan, only the most major streets have names.

— PLANET TOKYO

In Italy, until recently, it was not possible to get a haircut on Monday.

— FINANCIAL TIMES, MARCH 28, 2007

In recent years, Japan, Argentina, and Brazil have legalized forms of incest.

— *THE GUARDIAN*, FEBRUARY 27, 2007

In 2003, Britain was responsible for 2.9 percent of global oil production, slightly less than Kuwait's 3.0 percent.

— *THE ECONOMIST*, NOVEMBER 7, 2004

In 2006, 24 percent of the world's construction cranes were operating in Dubai.

— *GULF NEWS*, JUNE 18, 2006

There were 487 homicides in Haiti in 2007, about 5.6 per 100,000 people. The Caribbean's average homicide rate is 30 per 100,000, making Haiti one of the safest places in the region.

— *THE WASHINGTON TIMES*, MARCH 8, 2008

Per capita sales of board games in Germany are higher than anywhere else in the world.

— *THE ECONOMIST*, FEBRUARY 19, 2005

The Dutch smoke more than anyone in the developed world—around one in three adults are regular smokers.

— *THE GUARDIAN*, JULY 30, 2005

HEAD, SHOULDERS, KNEES, AND TOES

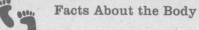

Facts About the Body

Bacteria account for 10 percent of our dry
body weight.   —CRISPIN TICKELL

!?!

The human spine flexes 100 million times in
fifty or sixty years.

—*THE SYDNEY MORNING HERALD,* OCTOBER 13, 2005

!?!

By the age of fifty, the human eye lets in 20
percent less light than at its peak.

—*LOS ANGELES TIMES,* FEBRUARY 17, 2004

!?!

Our eyes are always the same size, but our
nose and ears never stop growing.

—BBC.CO.UK

!?!

It is possible to donate half a liver.

—BBC.CO.UK

!?!

Of the trillions of cells in a typical human
body, only about one in ten is human. The
rest are microbial.

—*THE NEW YORK TIMES MAGAZINE,* AUGUST 13, 2006

 # Sobering Thoughts

Facts About Drinking and Alcohol

London has 13 percent of Britain's population but just 9 percent of its pubs.

—LONDONIST.COM, AUGUST 20, 2007

A man-sized rat could drink twelve bottles of scotch a day with no more liver damage than a human would have from half a bottle a day.

—NATIONAL ANTI-VIVISECTION SOCIETY

In Britain, drinking alcohol is a factor in more than half of violent crimes and a third of domestic violence incidents.

—*BMJ*, DECEMBER 2007

Austin, Texas, is the hardest-drinking city in America. 61.5 percent of adult residents say they have had at least one drink of alcohol within the past thirty days, and 20.6 percent of respondents confess to binge drinking, or having five or more drinks on one occasion.
—*FORBES*, AUGUST 7, 2008

The poet laureate of the United Kingdom is entitled to "a butt of sack per annum"—110 gallons of Spanish sherry, or about 630 bottles, each year.
—*PROSPECT* RESEARCH

China drinks far more beer than any other nation. Snow, China's most popular beer, commands only about 5 percent of the domestic market.
—ECONOMIST.COM, OCTOBER 16, 2007

In the United States, 12 percent of Coca-Cola is consumed with or for breakfast.
—*THE GREAT FOOD ALMANAC* BY IRENA CHALMERS

In 2003, Russians bought more beer than vodka for
the first time ever. — BUSINESS ANALYTICA

❗

In 1954, Bob Hawke, future Australian prime minister, earned a place in the *Guinness Book of Records*
by drinking two-and-a-half pints—a "yard"—of beer
in eleven seconds.

— EVERYTHING YOU DIDN'T NEED TO KNOW
ABOUT AUSTRALIA BY ADAM WARD

❓

By the late 1970s, Kingsley Amis was spending
£1,000 a month on scotch.

— BOOKFORUM, FEBRUARY/MARCH 2008

❗

In 2006, the average Russian drank twenty-six pints
of alcohol—three times as much as in 1990, and
more than half as much again as in 2005. Alcohol
was responsible for 28,386 deaths—12 percent of the
Russian total—but this represented a fall from
2005's number of 40,877. — PHYSORG.COM

❓

On average, ten cars a day emerging from English Channel crossings break down owing to the weight of the duty-free alcohol they carry.

—DRIVING STANDARDS AGENCY, 2005

Vietnam is the second largest producer of coffee in the world, after Brazil. It produces twenty times as much as Uganda.

—*PROSPECT* RESEARCH

In the United States, the price of a bottle of Coca-Cola remained the same—5 cents—from 1886 to 1959.

—SLATE, MAY 11, 2007

The average person in Luxembourg drinks 27.3 liters of alcohol a year—more than in any other country.

—WORLD HEALTH ORGANIZATION

Starbucks bought 37 percent of Costa Rica's entire coffee crop in the 2004–05 season.

—*THE ECONOMIST,* APRIL 1, 2006

The Coca-Cola brand is estimated to be worth $67 billion, making it the most valuable in the world.

—B2B INTERNATIONAL

Twenty-one percent of the calories consumed by an average American come from beverages.

— *THE NEW YORK TIMES,* MARCH 27, 2007

Advertising wine is banned on French television.

—BBC.CO.UK, FEBRUARY 27, 2007

Australia and New Zealand have approximately 850 people to each espresso machine, a ratio bested only by Italy. In the United States, there are roughly 20,000 people per espresso machine.

—COFFEEGEEK.COM, JUNE 12, 2007

In Scotland, the most popular soft drink is Irn-Bru—making it the only nation in the world where neither Coca-Cola nor Pepsi occupies the top spot.   —BBC

China is the world's sixth-largest wine producer.

—SLATE, AUGUST 8, 2008

Red Bull is illegal in Norway, Denmark, and Iceland.

—*PROSPECT* RESEARCH

Chow Down

Facts About Food

Henry David Thoreau once burned down three hundred acres of forest trying to cook a fish he had caught for supper. *—THE TIMES*, APRIL 17, 2003

In 1997 and 1998, olive oil was the most adulterated agricultural product in the European Union, prompting the Union's antifraud office to establish an olive oil task force.

—THE NEW YORKER, AUGUST 13, 2007

Peaches and almonds are both part of the rose family.

—CANBERRA TIMES, MARCH 12, 2000

Those who eat with one other person consume about
35 percent more than when they are alone; members
of a group of four eat about 75 percent more; those
in groups of seven or more eat 96 percent more.

— *THE NEW REPUBLIC,* MARCH 22, 2007

There are 40,000 Chinese restaurants in the United
States—more than the number of McDonald's,
Burger Kings, and KFCs combined.

— *THE FORTUNE COOKIE CHRONICLES: ADVENTURES IN
THE WORLD OF CHINESE FOOD* BY JENNIFER 8 LEE

Serbia produces almost a third of the world's rasp-
berries. — U.S. DEPARTMENT OF AGRICULTURE

Britain is responsible for half the potato chip con-
sumption of Europe. — BBC RADIO 4, MAY 15, 2006

In 2006, McDonald's sales in France grew by 8 percent, almost double the growth in America.

— *THE NEW YORK SUN*, JULY 2, 2007

In 1978, the average French meal lasted 82 minutes. Today it is around 38 minutes.

— *MICROTRENDS* BY MARK J. PENN

Michelin recently launched a guide to Tokyo dining. It awarded more stars to restaurants in the Japanese capital (191) than to any other city in the world. Paris got 64 and New York 42.

— *FINANCIAL TIMES*, NOVEMBER 19, 2007

Switzerland imports 24 percent of the world's caviar.

—WORLD WILDLIFE FUND

Parmesan cheese accounts for 10 percent of thefts from Italian shops—more than any other item.

— *THE SUNDAY TELEGRAPH*, NOVEMBER 5, 2006

68   YOU ARE ONE-THIRD daffodil

Q

The Finns spend more on ice cream than any other
European culture, averaging $110 a head in 2005—
just beating the Italians. Britons spend less than
half that figure. —EUROMONITOR INTERNATIONAL

Q

The Japanese consume almost a third of all the fish
eaten in the world. —*PROSPECT* RESEARCH

The Birds and the Bees

Facts About Sex

One British woman in four prefers gardening to sex.

— NEWEDEN.CO.UK

On an average day, about 3.3 percent of the world's population has sex. Less than 0.4 percent of these acts of copulation results in a birth.

— WORLD HEALTH ORGANIZATION

The clitoris has eight thousand nerve fibers, which is more than the fingertips and tongue, and twice the number in the penis.

— *FINANCIAL TIMES*, MARCH 24, 2001

Six percent of all heart attacks occur during sexual intercourse. Of these, 90 percent happen during extramarital sex.

— *THE GOLDEN AGE IS IN US* BY ALEXANDER COCKBURN

A survey in Melbourne found that mild to moderately depressed women enjoy a third more sex than the nondepressed. — *HERALD SUN,* MARCH 20, 2008

Fourteen percent of U.S. teenagers who call themselves "evangelical" or "born again" have had three or more sexual partners by age seventeen, compared to 9 percent of those who call themselves mainstream Protestants.

— *FORBIDDEN FRUIT: SEX & RELIGION IN THE LIVES OF AMERICAN TEENAGERS* BY MARK REGNERUS

The average Japanese person has sex forty-five times a year, compared with the global average of 103.

— *THE JAPAN TIMES,* JUNE 22, 2006

In the United States, adult bookshops outnumber
McDonald's restaurants three to one.

—EFFECT OF PORNOGRAPHY ON WOMEN AND CHILDREN,

U.S. SENATE JUDICIARY COMMITTEE

In China, on average, people do not exchange their
first kiss until the age of twenty-three.

— THE SUNDAY TIMES, JUNE 10, 2007

In 2006, General Motors' health-care responsibilities
made it the largest private purchaser of Viagra in
the world. It spent $17 million on the pills.

—CONSUMERAFFAIRS.COM, APRIL 18, 2006

Napoleon often masturbated before going into battle.

— THE GUARDIAN, MAY 31, 2008

In Newfoundland, one in six people say they have
had a "ghost-rape" experience.

—SEX AND THE PARANORMAL BY PAUL CHAMBERS

The average male orgasm lasts eight seconds, the average female orgasm twenty seconds.

— *THE OBSERVER*, FEBRUARY 11, 2001

About 41 percent of Chinese schedule sex, versus only 3 percent of Russians and 7 percent of Americans.

— *BUSINESSWEEK*, MAY 10, 2007

Forty-seven percent of British men and 35 percent of women say they would give up sex for six months in exchange for a 50-inch plasma HD television. But only 17 percent of men would stop watching soccer.

— *THE REGISTER*, FEBRUARY 11, 2008

LIKE A HORSE AND CARRIAGE
Facts About Marriage

Fifty-seven percent of marriages in Sudan, 50 percent in Pakistan, and 36 percent in Saudi Arabia are between first cousins.

— *AFTER THE EMPIRE* BY EMMANUEL TODD

!?!

The Indian government will give $250 in cash, plus a certificate of appreciation, to anyone who marries a Dalit, or "untouchable." — *LOS ANGELES TIMES*, NOVEMBER 4, 2007

!?!

In 1900, it was made illegal in Iran for local women to marry Afghan men.

— *PROSPECT* RESEARCH

!?!

In Kansas and Massachusetts, the minimum age for marriage is twelve.

— *CHICAGO TRIBUNE*, DECEMBER 11, 2004

!?!

In the United States, 36 percent of newlywed couples have already had a physically violent argument. —EDGE.ORG

!?!

A poll of 10,000 American married couples in 2006 and 2007 found that 19 percent met online, compared to 17 percent who got together at work and 17 percent who met through friends.

—*DAILY MIRROR*, AUGUST 14, 2008

The Games People Play

Facts About Sports

On average, countries that win the World Cup add 0.7 percent to their economic growth that year.

—ABN AMRO

Of the 10,500 athletes who competed in the 2004 Olympics, only eleven were openly gay.

—OUTSPORTS.COM

Every week, ten times more people in China watch English Premier League soccer than in Britain.

—*THE GUARDIAN*, JANUARY 19, 2008

Senegal's only athlete at the 2006 Winter Olympics, Leyti Seck, who competed as an alpine skier, was brought up in Austria and had never been to Senegal.

—REUTERS

The 2006 World Cup final had a higher U.S. television audience than the 2006 World Series.

— *THE NEW REPUBLIC*, JULY 17, 2007

All eight members of the Qatari weightlifting team at the 2000 Olympics were originally Bulgarian.

— *THE GUARDIAN*, SEPTEMBER 27, 2000

The address of the Australian Broadcasting Corporation in every Australian state capital city is P.O. Box 9994, after Sir Don Bradman's test cricket batting average of 99.94.   — *AUSTRALIA* BY PHILLIP KNIGHTLEY

650,000 people in South Korea have Manchester
United credit cards.

—*INTERNATIONAL HERALD TRIBUNE,* APRIL 15, 2007

Ⓠ

The Chicago White Sox start their midweek games
at 7:11 P.M., thanks to a sponsorship deal with 7-
Eleven stores.   —*THE GUARDIAN,* OCTOBER 20, 2006

Ⓠ

China won sixty-three medals at the 2004 Olympics,
thirty-two of them gold. India won just one: a silver
in shooting.   —*PROSPECT,* DECEMBER 2007

Ⓠ

In March 2009, the North Korean women's soccer
team was ranked fifth in the world.

—*PROSPECT* RESEARCH

Ⓠ

At the 2004 Olympics, the Bahamas won just over
six medals per million population—almost three
times as many as any other country.

—ECONOMIST.COM, JUNE 3, 2008

New York's department of education has set up a cricket league, with about six hundred secondary school students playing. It is the only public school system in America to offer competitive cricket.

— *THE DAILY TELEGRAPH*, APRIL 7, 2008

In 1974, Leicestershire golfer Bob Taylor achieved three holes-in-one in competition over three successive days, on the same hole.

— *HOLE IN ONE*, BY CHRIS RODELL

The average participant in the New York City marathon has an annual household income of $130,000.

— *THE NEW YORKER*, AUGUST 11, 2008

With 800 million players, beach volleyball is the second most popular sport in the world by participation, after soccer.

—BBC1

Cheerleading has accounted for 65 percent of all cat-astrophic sports injuries among high school females over the past twenty-five years.

—LIVESCIENCE.COM, AUGUST 11, 2008

The marathon is the only Olympic distance track event never to have been won by a Kenyan.

— *THE NEW YORKER,* AUGUST, 2008

When India's Sachin Tendulkar batted against Pak-istan in test cricket matches, the television audience in India exceeded the total population of Europe.

— *THE OBSERVER,* JANUARY 11, 2004

Workin' 9–5

Facts About Jobs and Careers

About two hundred people around the world make a living by designing typefaces.

— *THE ATLANTIC*, JANUARY/FEBRUARY 2008

There are more African scientists and engineers working in the United States than in Africa.

—U.K. COMMISSION FOR AFRICA REPORT, 2005

There are as many fake doctors practicing in India as real ones.

— *HARPER'S*, MAY 2008

More than 30 percent of the technology firms created in Silicon Valley since the 1980s were founded
by entrepreneurs with Indian or Chinese roots.

— *THE ECONOMIST,* MAY 6, 2006

?

Twenty percent of a British police officer's average
working day is spent filling out forms.

— *DAILY MAIL,* FEBRUARY 21, 2008

!

In 1983, Los Angeles had three times as many workers in the aerospace industry than the movie industry. By 2000, the proportions had reversed.

— *PROSPECT,* MARCH 2004

?

About 25 percent of American workers in the private sector get no paid holiday at all.

— *THE NEW REPUBLIC,* JULY 30, 2007

!

The average British commute is one hour and five
minutes. In 2003, it was thirty-five minutes.

— *THE GUARDIAN,* JANUARY 21, 2008

Ninety percent of American firms are family-owned, and around a third of Fortune 500 companies are at least partly family-managed. Family businesses account for two-thirds of employment in the European Union.

— *EUROPEAN UNION DYNASTIES: FORTUNES AND MISFORTUNES OF THE WORLD'S GREAT FAMILY BUSINESSES* BY DAVID S. LANDES

The Mafia accounts for 7 percent of Italian GDP, more than any single business.

— *LOS ANGELES TIMES,* APRIL 13, 2008

Until 1977, German men had the legal right to forbid their wives from taking paid employment.

— *THE END OF MASCULINITY* BY JOHN MACINNES

About 25 percent of the Norwegian workforce is absent from work on any given day.

— *DISCOVER YOUR INNER ECONOMIST* BY TYLER COWEN

Forty percent of Americans polled in May 2006 said they had no plans to take a summer holiday.

—THE CONFERENCE BOARD

In 1983, a Soviet factory made 13,000 pairs of sunglasses so dark that wearers could look directly at the sun and not see it. —ITAR-TASS NEWS AGENCY

About 30 percent of the Danish workforce changes jobs every year.

— THE WALL STREET JOURNAL, APRIL 25, 2007

One in three Italians finds a job through a relative.

— THE NEW YORK TIMES, AUGUST 23, 2006

The average working week in South Korea is over forty-five hours, nearly seven hours longer than any other OECD country. —ECONOMIST.COM, APRIL 16, 2008

By late 1967, the five thousand workers at Egypt's
El Nasr automotive plant were producing an average of two vehicles a week.

— SIX DAYS OF WAR BY MICHAEL OREN

❓

The ratio of workers to retirees in the United States
in 1950 was 18 to 1. In 2050, it is projected to be
2 to 1. But in 2050, the worker-to-*dependent* ratio
will be 10 to 8—better than in the 1960s, when it
was 10 to 9. *— PROSPECT,* FEBRUARY 2008

❗

Eight-and-a-half percent of American CEOs live on a
golf course.

— SAN JOSE MERCURY NEWS, APRIL 12, 2007

❓

The unemployment rate in Brussels is 17 percent.

— GLOBAL POST, APRIL 21, 2009

❗

The salary of Ireland's prime minister, or Taoiseach,
is 310,000 euros—more than almost any other world
leader. —ECONOMIST.COM, NOVEMBER 1, 2007

In 1940, 58 percent of black women with jobs worked as maids. Now only 1 percent do.

—THE ECONOMIST, AUGUST 4, 2005

❶

In 1990, only nineteen companies from the developing world made the Fortune 500 list of the top global firms. In 2005, the figure had risen to forty-seven.

—THE WILSON QUARTERLY, SPRING 2008

❷

Thirty-five percent of American and 20 percent of British entrepreneurs are dyslexic. But only 1 percent of corporate managers in the United States have dyslexia.

—THE NEW YORK TIMES, DECEMBER 6, 2007

❶

In São Paulo, 10 percent of all homicides are committed by police officers.

—VEJA

❷

There are more Ethiopian doctors practicing in Chicago than in Ethiopia.

—THE ECONOMIST, JANUARY 3, 2008

❶

The nine highest-paying jobs in the United States
are in the medical profession. Anesthesiologists are
the highest paid (with a mean annual salary of
$184,340), with surgeons second. The only nonmed-
ical occupations in the top fifteen are chief executives (tenth) and airline pilots (fourteenth). Lawyers
are sixteenth highest. Restaurant worker is the
worst-paid job, with a mean annual salary of
$15,930.   —*FORBES*, JUNE 4, 2007

❷

Indians account for 38 percent of doctors in the
United States, 36 percent of scientists at NASA, and
34 percent of employees at Microsoft, 28 percent at
IBM, 17 percent at Intel, and 13 percent at Xerox.
                                    —*THE TIMES OF INDIA*, MARCH 11, 2008

❶

New York City's police force is nearly four times bigger than America's entire border patrol.
                                    —*THE ECONOMIST*, APRIL 1, 2006

❷

For 2007, UPS redesigned its routes to reduce left-hand turns. As a result, the company shaved 30 million miles off its deliveries that year.

—*PARADE*, APRIL 6, 2008

Ninety-five percent of filed documents remain filed forever.

—*FASTER* BY JAMES GLEICK

Intel employees collectively send or read 3 million emails a day.

—*THE NEW YORK TIMES*, MARCH 2, 2008

Police officers in Los Angeles are more likely to take their own life than to be killed by a criminal. Nineteen Los Angeles police officers killed themselves between 1998 and 2007, while only seven died in the line of duty.

—*LOS ANGELES TIMES*, MARCH 26, 2008

In 1935, 7.5 percent of Germans were members of the Nazi party, but among teachers the figure was nearly one-third.

—*THE SCOTSMAN*, AUGUST 13, 2007

Q

Between one-third and one-half of the developing
world's science and technology workers live in the
west.   —INSTITUTE FOR PUBLIC POLICY RESEARCH

Q

Forty-one percent of British full-time employees
work over forty hours a week, compared to 16 percent in France and 9 percent in Sweden.

—EUROSTAT

Q

The average employee will write 50,000 lists of
things to do during the course of their working life
and receive more than 320,000 emails.

—*THE DAILY TELEGRAPH*, SEPTEMBER 1, 2008

Q

Two out of five office workers have an intimate ro-
mance with a colleague.

—*DAILY TELEGRAPH*, SEPTEMBER 1, 2008

Q

Of the 483 people who had been launched into space as of March 2008, eighteen died during the mission. This mortality rate of 3.74 percent makes astronaut one of the most dangerous professions: compare with a 0.39 percent mortality rate among the U.S. military in Iraq from 2003 to 2006, and 2.18 percent in Vietnam from 1966 to 1972.

— *THE SPACE REVIEW*, MAY 17, 2008

Hit the Books

Facts About Education

Asians make up 35 percent of the undergraduate body at MIT but only 4 percent of the U.S. population.

— *THE NEW YORK REVIEW OF BOOKS*, NOVEMBER 3, 2005

One in three school-age girls in Turkey does not attend school. In the Kurdish region, only 14 percent of girls attend secondary school.

— *THE ECONOMIST*, JULY 29, 2006

Only 16 percent of Germans hold a university degree, about the same proportion as Turks and Mexicans.

—OECD

In the United States in 2002, only six undergraduates earned Arabic language degrees.

—SLATE, OCTOBER 4, 2004

Britain and Iceland are the only two developed countries in which schoolchildren can stop studying history at the age of fourteen. —BBC.CO.UK, JANUARY 27, 2005

In China and Japan, 59 percent and 66 percent of undergraduates respectively receive their degrees in science and engineering, compared with 32 percent in the United States.

—THE WASHINGTON POST, DECEMBER 6, 2006

In the United States, 75 percent of money given away by philanthropists goes to higher education.

—ANTHONY GIDDENS

There are ten applicants for every place on teacher-training courses in Finnish universities.

—THE WASHINGTON POST, AUGUST 7, 2005

In the United States, more students learn Latin than Russian, Japanese, Italian, Mandarin, and Cantonese combined.
— *PROSPECT* RESEARCH

About 70 percent of Chinese students who leave to study abroad don't return.
— RICHARD SPENCER, *DAILY TELEGRAPH* BLOG, JUNE 15, 2007

In the United States, more bachelor's degrees are awarded every year in parks, recreation, leisure, and fitness studies than in all foreign languages and literatures combined.
— *THE NEW YORKER*, MAY 21, 2007

Ninety-six percent of Jamaicans who receive an advanced education emigrate.
— *FOREIGN POLICY*, SEPTEMBER/OCTOBER 2004

The percentage of new recruits to the U.S. Army with high-school diplomas fell from 94 percent in 2003 to 71 percent in 2007.

—SLATE, JANUARY 24, 2008

❗

In 1976, the United States had 30 percent of the world's college students. By 2006, that had dropped to 14 percent. —BUSINESS REPORT, JUNE 25, 2007

❓

Doubling the number of engineering students in the United States would increase GDP by 0.5 percent, while doubling the number studying law would cause a 0.3 percent drop.

—THE ECONOMIST, JULY 13, 2005

❗

Ten years after graduation, 44 percent of 1980 female Harvard graduates who had married kept their own name, while just 32 percent of 1990 graduates kept theirs. —HARVARD GAZETTE, AUGUST 26, 2004

❓

In 2007, Harvard accepted only 9 percent of under-graduate applicants, the lowest figure in its history, and down from 18 percent in 1983.

— REASON, MAY 21, 2007

In 1968, France had 605,000 university students—as many as Britain, West Germany, and Belgium combined.

— THE INDEPENDENT MAGAZINE, FEBRUARY 23, 2008

Of the nineteen presidents since 1900, only eight went to Ivy League institutions as undergraduates. Harry Truman never went to college at all.

— TIMES LITERARY SUPPLEMENT, JULY 12, 2006

In 2006, four of the five richest Americans—Bill Gates, casino owner Sheldon Adelson, Oracle's Larry Ellison, and Microsoft co-founder Paul Allen—were college dropouts. (The exception was Warren Buffett).

— ALL THE MONEY IN THE WORLD: HOW THE FORBES 400
MAKE—AND SPEND—THEIR FORTUNES BY
PETER W. BERNSTEIN AND ANNALYN SWAN

In Germany, only 13.5 percent of children under three attend nursery school, compared with the European average of 35 percent.

—EXPATICA, MAY 15, 2007

❶

The United States is home to 4 percent of the global population age 5 to 25, but accounts for more than a quarter of the global public education budget. It spends as much as the Middle East, central and eastern Europe, central Asia, Latin America, the Caribbean, south and west Asia, and sub-Saharan Africa combined.

—UNESCO

❷

The average IQ in Germany is 107, the highest in Europe. Serbs have the lowest IQ, with an average of 89.

—THE TIMES, MARCH 27, 2006

❶

There are nearly 200,000 students at Cairo University.

—THE NEW YORKER, JUNE 2, 2008

EUREKA!
Facts About Inventions

Thomas Jefferson invented the swivel chair.

—*HOUSTON CHRONICLE*, FEBRUARY 18, 2006

!?!

The philosopher Daniel Dennett introduced the Frisbee to Britain.

—*THE OBSERVER*, MARCH 12, 2006

!?!

Isaac Newton invented the cat door.

—SCIENCE MUSEUM

!?!

A third of patent applications in America in 1905 were related to the bicycle.

—*RSA JOURNAL*, WINTER 2005

!?!

The length of time from invention to application of the ballpoint pen was fifty-eight years; for the zipper, it was thirty-two years.

—U.K. DEPARTMENT OF TRADE AND INDUSTRY

!?!

The United States grants 78 percent more high-tech patents per capita than Europe.

— *TIME*, JANUARY 19, 2004

!?!

Per capita, Cuba grants more patents than either China or India.

—ECONOMIST.COM, JULY 30, 2007

!?!

Windshield wipers, laser printers, and bulletproof vests were all invented by women.

—BRITISH ASSOCIATION FOR THE
ADVANCEMENT OF SCIENCE

!?!

Ninety-five percent of all patent applications in the United States are approved, compared with just 65 percent in Europe and Japan.

— *THE NEW YORKER*, DECEMBER 26, 2005

What a Wonderful World

Facts to Cheer You Up

Kabul's population has increased from 300,000 in 2001 to 3 million today.

— FINANCIAL TIMES, FEBRUARY 11, 2008

Between 1989 and 2005, the number of incidences of mass killings of civilians around the world decreased by 90 percent.

— THE NEW REPUBLIC, MARCH 22, 2007

In India, 127 million people were vaccinated against polio in a single day in 1997.

—WORLD HEALTH ORGANIZATION

In 2005, 71 percent of email users said they had received pornographic email spam. In 2007, the num-
ber was 52 percent.   —PEW RESEARCH CENTER

●

Since 1990, the average American has added about
two and a half years to his life, but the average New
Yorker has added 6.2 years. In the year 2004 alone,
New Yorkers' life expectancy shot up by five months.

—*NEW YORK*, AUGUST 20, 2007

●

In the United States, the total number of cancer
deaths dropped in 2003 for the first time since
records began in 1930. The biggest cause was a decline in the number of smokers.

—*NEW SCIENTIST*, FEBRUARY 18, 2006

●

In December 2006, 65 percent of Iranians had a very
unfavorable view of the United States. By April
2008, this had fallen to 51 percent.

—WORLDPUBLICOPINION.ORG

●

August 2006 marked one thousand days of peace between nations—the longest period since the Second
World War.

— *THE CHRISTIAN SCIENCE MONITOR*, AUGUST 30, 2006

In 1895, 5 percent of Britain was covered in wood-
land; by 2003, the figure was 11.8 percent.

— *THE OBSERVER*, JANUARY 26, 2003

Between 1962 and 2002, life expectancy in the Middle East and North Africa increased from around
forty-eight years to sixty-nine—the strongest per-
formance of any region in the world.

—CHARLES KENNY

There are nearly as many American Indians in California now as there were in the eighteenth century.

— *THE NEW YORK REVIEW OF BOOKS*, OCTOBER 7, 2004

Don't Tell Me That!

Facts You'd Rather Not Know.

Facial herpes—or "scrum pox"—is common among the forwards in a rugby team.

—STUDENTHEALTH.CO.UK

The U.S. government's terrorist watch list contains around 755,000 names.

—CNN, OCTOBER 25, 2007

By 2007, the cost of a coffin in Baghdad was fifty to seventy-five dollars, up from five to ten dollars before the Iraq war.

—*THE WASHINGTON POST*, NOVEMBER 18, 2007

Ten percent of the flow of China's Yellow River is
raw sewage.

—INSTITUTE OF PUBLIC AND ENVIRONMENTAL AFFAIRS

There are an estimated 10,000 trillion ants on
earth—roughly 1.6 million for each human. Their
combined weight is equivalent to that of the entire
human population.

—MSN

There are 67 million rats in Britain—1.2 rats for
every person.

—BBC1

Every day, five U.S. soldiers try to kill themselves.
Before the Iraq war, there was less than one suicide
attempt a day.

—CNN.COM, FEBRUARY 3, 2008

An asteroid large enough to wipe out France came
within 800,000 kilometers of hitting Earth in August
2001; it was spotted only days before it hurtled past.

— TIME, JANUARY 21, 2002

Eighty percent of cancer cases are caused by environmental factors.

— *LIVING DOWNSTREAM* BY SANDRA STEINGRABER

Pneumonia kills more children worldwide than any other illness—and more than AIDS, malaria, and measles combined.

— UNICEF

Almost two-thirds of Palestinians think violence has achieved more than negotiations.

— PALESTINIAN CENTER FOR POLICY AND SURVEY RESEARCH

A third of the world's obese people live in developing countries.

— *50 FACTS THAT SHOULD CHANGE THE WORLD*
BY JESSICA WILLIAMS

More than half the organs used in transplant surgery in China come from judicial executions.

— *HUMAN RIGHTS WATCH WORLD REPORT 2007*

About 90 percent of the planet's disease burden falls on poor countries. Just 3 percent of drug company R&D is aimed at such diseases.

— *THE ECONOMIST,* APRIL 16, 2005

There are more than one thousand chemicals in coffee. Twenty-seven of these were tested on rodents; nineteen were found to be carcinogenic.

— BBC RADIO 4

Under Gorbachev, 5 percent of senior Soviet officials had a background in the armed forces or security services. Under Putin, the figure for Russian officials was 78 percent.

— *HARPER'S,* MAY 2007

Half of all Australians will contract skin cancer at some point in their lives.

— *SUNDAY TIMES,* APRIL 11, 2004

New Zealand's child murder rate is 0.9 per 100,000 children, the third worst in the OECD. The overall murder rate is 2.5 per 100,000 people.

— THE TIMES, AUGUST 7, 2006

There were 658 suicide bombings around the world in 2007—more than double the number in any of the previous twenty-five years. Afghanistan and Iraq were responsible for 542 of these.

— THE WASHINGTON POST, APRIL 18, 2008

In a 2002 survey, 52 percent of Russians said they thought America "got what it deserved" on 9/11.

— THE TIMES, SEPTEMBER 12, 2002

When Tony Blair came to power in Britain in 1997, there were 129 shoplifters in prison; when he left in 2007, there were 1,400. In 1997, there were fewer than 4,000 life prisoners; in 2007, there were 6,431—more than in Germany, France, Italy, and Turkey combined. — *THE GUARDIAN,* JUNE 20, 2007

Q

In New Zealand, because of male emigration, a thirty-two-year-old woman has as much chance of finding a partner her age as does an eighty-two-year-old woman. —POPULATION GROWTH REPORT 2005

!

One in five British children cannot name an activity they have done with their fathers in the past week. One-third of all children never see their absent parent following family breakdown.
—NATIONAL SOCIETY FOR THE PREVENTION OF CRUELTY TO CHILDREN

Q

One in four adults in New York City has herpes.
—*USA TODAY,* JUNE 9, 2008

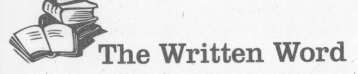

The Written Word

Facts About Literature and Writing

As of late 2007, *The New York Times* had forty blogs. 　　　　　　　　　　　　　　—GAWKER.COM

The number of children attending hospital emergency departments in the UK dropped by almost half on the weekends when new Harry Potter books were published. 　　—*DAILY TELEGRAPH*, JULY 15, 2007

Mark Twain's *Life on the Mississippi* (1883) was the first published novel to have been written on a typewriter. The machine, a Sholes and Glidden, typed in capital letters only. 　　　　　—EARTHLINK.NET

Three-quarters of all Oscar-winning films have been
literary adaptations. —*PROSPECT,* MARCH 2003

The first edition of Freud's *The Interpretation of
Dreams* (1899) sold only 351 copies in its first six
years. —*PROSPECT,* OCTOBER 2005

Five years after the 2001 terrorist attacks on New
York and Washington, 1,248 books about 9/11 had
been published. —*THE INDEPENDENT,* SEPTEMBER 11, 2006

In 2003, in the week of National Poetry Day in the
UK, poetry sales fell by 10 percent from the previous
week. —*THE GUARDIAN,* OCTOBER 18, 2003

More than 150 books have the words "before you
die" in their titles. —AMAZON.COM

Charles Dickens created 989 named characters.

— *THE GUARDIAN*, MARCH 25, 2006

The Purpose Driven Life, a Christian advice book published in 2002, is the bestselling hardcover in U.S. history. Over 25 million copies have been sold.

— *THE ECONOMIST*, DECEMBER 3, 2005

In the UK, *Harry Potter and the Half-Blood Prince* sold more copies on one day in 2005 than Dan Brown's *The Da Vinci Code* did the whole year.

— *THE INDEPENDENT*, JUNE 10, 2007

Mein Kampf was the second-bestselling book in Turkey in March 2005.

— *HARPER'S*, JUNE 2005

Only half of American adults have read a book since leaving high school.

— RANDOM HOUSE

Five of the ten bestselling novels in Japan in 2007 were written on mobile phones.

— THE ECONOMIST, APRIL 10, 2008

About 80 percent of all news on the Internet originates from print newspapers.

— THE NEW YORK REVIEW OF BOOKS, AUGUST 16, 2007

There have been more translations of Kant into Persian over the last decade than into any other language.

— NEW REPUBLIC, JUNE 1, 2006

From 1945 to 1955, Britain's bestselling book was E.V. Rieu's translation of *The Odyssey*.

— THE GUARDIAN, JANUARY 24, 2005

In 1893, when Arthur Conan Doyle killed off Sherlock Holmes, 20,000 people cancelled their subscriptions to *The Strand Magazine*, which had published the Holmes stories.   *— THE WILSON QUARTERLY, SUMMER 1999*

The Da Vinci Code is the bestselling book in French history. A quarter of the population is estimated to have read it.   —*BUSINESSWEEK*, MAY 17, 2006

In central London in the late seventeenth century, post was delivered ten to twelve times a day.
                    —*AT LARGE AND AT SMALL: CONFESSIONS OF A*
                    LITERARY HEDONIST BY ANNE FADIMAN

Around 200,000 academic journals are published in the English language. The average number of readers per article is five.   —*PROSPECT* RESEARCH

Thirty percent of published hardcover books go directly from the printer to the remainder warehouse.
                    —*THE DAILY TELEGRAPH*, AUGUST 31, 2002

The word "bible" does not appear in the works of Shakespeare.   —*THE GUARDIAN*, MARCH 3, 2006

The eighteenth-century scholar Edmond Malone calculated that 4,144 of the 6,033 lines in parts I, II, and III of *Henry VI* were plagiarized by Shakespeare.

—*EX LIBRIS* BY ANNE FADIMAN

In academic publishing, each additional self-citation by an author increases the number of citations from others after one year by about one, and by about three after five years.

—*SCIENTOMETRICS*

Goethe's *Faust* is 12,111 lines long. The full text of *Hamlet* is 3,800.

—*PROSPECT,* JUNE 2001

The record for the highest number of short stories published in *The New Yorker* by an author in one year is held by E.B. White (twenty-eight in 1927). The overall record is held by James Thurber, who published 273 stories from 1927 to 1961.

—EMDASHES.COM, OCTOBER 16, 2006

The Japanese national anthem is only five lines long. The words were taken from a tenth-century anthology of poetry. The translation is: "May the reign of the emperor / continue for a thousand, nay, eight thousand generations / and for the eternity that it takes / for small pebbles to grow into a great rock / and become covered with moss."   —ABOUT.COM

Global newspaper sales rose by over 9 percent between 2002 and 2007.   — *THE OBSERVER*, JUNE 10, 2007

Shakespeare used a total of 31,534 different words in his works, although 14,376 appeared only once.

— *PROSPECT*, JULY 2004

This Is How We Do It

Facts About How We Live Today

Fifty percent of speaking time consists of silence.

— *THE NEW YORK TIMES,* JANUARY 3, 2004

Half of British women own more than thirty pairs of shoes.　　　　— *THE GUARDIAN,* AUGUST 19, 2006

In the United States, half of all children age four to six have played video games, and a quarter say they do so regularly.

— *THE BOSTON GLOBE MAGAZINE,* FEBRUARY 20, 2005

The most expensive age of your life is thirty-four.

—*THE GUARDIAN*, AUGUST 19, 2006

Ten percent of people are left-handed and 20 percent are left-footed.

—*RIGHT HAND, LEFT HAND* BY CHRIS MCMANUS

Twenty-one percent of Americans say they are regularly "bored out of their mind," and 3.8 percent have sought counseling for boredom.

—*THE ATLAS OF EXPERIENCE* BY LOUISE VAN SWAAIJ
AND JEAN KLARE

In the United States, the lifetime cost to parents of rearing one middle-class child is about $1.43 million.

—*FAMILY BUSINESS*, EDITED BY HELEN WILKINSON

In any conversation lasting ten minutes or longer, 20 percent of adults will lie.

—*CALIFORNIA*, JULY/AUGUST 2007

There are half a million semiautomatic machine guns in Swiss homes.

—*50 FACTS YOU NEED TO KNOW: EUROPE* BY EMMA HARTLEY

In Britain, 93 percent of young people can master a computer game while only 38 percent can bake a potato.

—CENTRE FOR FOOD POLICY

Women are estimated to buy 80 percent of everything that is sold.

—*THE WHOLE WOMAN* BY GERMAINE GREER

Rents in central Manchester, a city in the northwest of England, are 40 percent higher than in central Manhattan.

—CENTRE FOR CITIES

Jews in Nice who want to buy a flat have to pay a fee of 900 to 7,000 euros to get around a Vichy law that is still on the books.

—*THE JERUSALEM POST,* MARCH 1, 2007

Between the year 2000 and the ship's retirement in
2008, the *Queen Elizabeth 2* had one full-time resi-
dent, an eighty-seven-year-old American widow who
lived in a modest, windowless cabin at a rent of
seven thousand dollars a month.

— THE TIMES, JUNE 2, 2008

By late 2006, only 35 percent of Americans had sent
a text message, compared to almost 100 percent of
Britons.   *— TECHNOLOGY REVIEW*, NOVEMBER 6, 2006

Between 2000 and 2005, the number of people in the
United States playing golf more than twenty-five
times a year fell by a third, from 6.9 million to 4.5
million.   *— THE NEW YORK TIMES*, FEBRUARY 21, 2008

In the United States, spending one's old age on
cruise ships is almost as cheap as care in an
assisted-living facility. The average cost for a person
to live on a cruise ship from 80 until death would be
$230,497, compared with $228,075 for care.

— JOURNAL OF THE AMERICAN GERIATRICS SOCIETY

❓

Women in almost every culture speak in deeper voices than Japanese women. American women's voices are lower than Japanese, Swedish women's lower than American, and Dutch women's lower than Swedish. — *THE HUMAN VOICE* BY ANNE KARPF

HOME SWEET HOME
Facts About the Places We Live In

Only 13 percent of Japanese homes have ever been resold, compared to 89 percent of homes in Britain and 78 percent in the United States. — *THE ECONOMIST*, JANUARY 3, 2008

!?!

During the 1950s, 20 percent of Americans changed residence every year and 6.9 percent moved across county borders. During the 1990s, the comparable figures were 17 percent and 6.6 percent.

— *PROSPECT* RESEARCH

!?!

One-third of all houses in Ireland were built in the last decade. — FINFACTS.COM

!?!

On average, Americans are more than four times as likely to move over the course of a year than the Japanese.

— SLATE, JULY 18, 2005

!?!

The average American two-car garage is 25 percent bigger than the average Tokyo home.

—*FAT, DUMB AND UGLY* BY PETER STRUPP

Brave New World

Facts About Technology and the Internet

Fewer than 1 percent of Google searches make use of the "I'm Feeling Lucky" button.

—PROSPECT, JANUARY 2004

There are fourteen countries in which there are more mobile phone subscriptions than there are people. The highest rate is in Luxembourg, where there are 157 subscribers for every 100 people. *—OECD*

More than half of Indians go online before leaving the house, while less than one-third of Americans or Canadians do. *—BUSINESSWEEK*, MAY 10, 2007

Spammers typically need to send one million emails
to get fifteen positive responses.

—THE NEW YORKER, AUGUST 6, 2007

An extra ten mobile phones per one hundred people
in a typical developing country leads to an additional 0.59 percentage points of growth in GDP per
person. *—THE ECONOMIST*, MAY 10, 2007

Fifty-two percent of Korean children between the
ages of three and five use the Internet. They spend
an average four hours a week online.

—THE KOREA HERALD, AUGUST 3, 2007

In 2007, YouTube consumed as much bandwidth as
the entire Internet did in 2000.

—THE NEW YORK TIMES, MARCH 13, 2008

When an unprotected PC running Windows goes online, there is a 50 percent chance it will be "compromised"—pick up a virus, spyware, or other malicious infection—within twelve minutes.

—SOPHOS

Q

British housewives spend 47 percent of their leisure time online, more than any other social group in the world. As a nation, the Chinese spend the largest fraction of their overall leisure time online.

— *THE GUARDIAN*, DECEMBER 31, 2008

Q

The United States accounts for 13 percent of all computer viruses and is the source of 15 percent of all spam, more than double its closest junk-mail rival, Turkey.

— *THE REGISTER*, FEBRUARY 29, 2008

Q

The total computing power at NASA at the time of Sputnik's launch in 1957 was far less than that available in a typical mobile phone today.

—MARTIN REES

Q

Boeing has a patent on using the gravity of the
moon to adjust the orbits of artificial satellites.

—SPACE-TRAVEL.COM, APRIL 11, 2008

Lights! Camera! Action!

Facts About Movies and Television

Three actors from the 1987 action film *Predator* have run for the office of governor, two successfully (Arnold Schwarzenegger in California and Jesse Ventura in Minnesota) and one unsuccessfully (Sonny Landham in Kentucky).

—*WEEKLY STANDARD*, AUGUST 18, 2003

In the United States, the visually impaired and blind watch television for an average twenty-four hours a week. The most popular programs are news shows, talk shows, and shopping channels.

—AMERICAN FOUNDATION FOR THE BLIND

Nollywood—Nigeria's film industry—produces more films a year than either Hollywood or Bollywood, and is the country's second largest employer.

—*PROSPECT*, APRIL 2007

While filming *Eyes Wide Shut*, Stanley Kubrick shot ninety-six takes of Tom Cruise walking through a door.

—BBC RADIO 3

Jack Bauer, the lead character from the series *24*, personally killed 112 people in the first five seasons of the show.

—*THE GUARDIAN*, JULY 8, 2006

Half the world's population has seen at least one of the seventeen James Bond films.

—PENGUIN

Adjusting for inflation, the most expensive film ever made is the 1963 version of *Cleopatra*, which cost almost $300 million in 2006 money.

—*THE NEW YORKER*, JANUARY 8, 2007

Only 4 percent of U.S. films are made by women,
compared with 25 percent in Iran.

— THE OBSERVER, JANUARY 18, 2004

There are no legal public cinemas in Saudi Arabia.

— INTERNATIONAL HERALD TRIBUNE, APRIL 29, 2006

Monty Python's Life of Brian was marketed in Sweden with the slogan, "The film that is so funny, it
was banned in Norway."

— IMDB.COM

The 1922 film *Nosferatu* credited sixteen people, *The
Matrix Revolutions* (2003) 701.

— THE OBSERVER BOOK OF FILM

Number of people killed per minute in the four
Rambo films: *Rambo: First Blood* (1982): 0.01;
Rambo: First Blood Part II (1985): 0.72; *Rambo III*
(1988): 1.30; *Rambo IV* (2008): 2.59.

— MARGINAL REVOLUTION, JANUARY 21, 2008

YOU ARE ONE-THIRD **daffodil**

The Czech Republic and Poland are the only two E.U. countries whose domestic films earn more overseas than the governments provide in subsidy to the film industry. —MARGINAL REVOLUTION, MAY 29, 2007

New Zealanders visit the cinema an average of eight times a year—more often than anyone else. The British make about three visits, Indians just one-and-a-half. —ECONOMIST.COM, MAY 31, 2007

Tune In

Facts About Music

One in every 3,400 Americans is an Elvis imperson-
ator. *—FINANCIAL TIMES*, JUNE 7, 2005

The musical comedy *You're a Good Man, Charlie
Brown*, based on the comic strip *Peanuts*, went
through 40,000 productions, involving 240,000 per-
formers. *—THE NEW YORKER*, OCTOBER 22, 2007

In the UK, the most effective musical deterrents to
loiterers and vandals are anything sung by
Pavarotti or written by Mozart.

—THE ECONOMIST, JANUARY 8, 2005

One in four British households owns a copy of Pink Floyd's *Dark Side of the Moon.*

— *THE GUARDIAN*, MARCH 3, 2006

Elgar is the only major composer to have mastered the bassoon. — *THE SPECTATOR*, JUNE 9, 2007

The top 100 bestselling albums in British history include no Rolling Stones, Bob Dylan, or Sex Pistols.

— *THE GUARDIAN*, NOVEMBER 16, 2006

In 2007, sales of physical music (mainly CDs) fell 19 percent in the United States.

— *THE ECONOMIST*, JANUARY 10, 2008

In 2004, 90 percent of the world's pianos were made in China, South Korea, or Japan.

— *THE INDEPENDENT*, OCTOBER 30, 2004

In 2006, sales of hip-hop albums fell in the United States by 33 percent—twice as much as the decline in CD sales overall. — *THE DAILY TELEGRAPH*, JULY 2, 2007

Analysis of forty-nine metropolitan areas in the United States shows that the greater the airtime devoted to country music, the greater the white suicide rate. The effect is independent of divorce, southernness, poverty, and gun availability.

—SCIENCEBLOGS.COM, DECEMBER 5, 2007

Romanians buy more compilation records, proportionally, than any other nationality. Such albums account for 41 percent of all music sales in Romania.

—IFPI

Aerosmith has made more money in royalties from the video game *Guitar Hero* than from any of its albums. —1UP.COM, SEPTEMBER 18, 2008

Q

From 1960 to 1974, 128 instrumental pieces of
music reached the top twenty in the United States,
while only thirty did from 1975 to 1990. Since then,
there have been just five.   —SLATE, MARCH 11, 2008

What's in a Name?

Facts About Titles and Monikers

About 85 percent of Chinese people share only a hundred surnames. Wang is the most popular (with 93 million people), followed by Li (92 million) and Zhang (88 million). At least 100,000 people are called "Wang Tao," making it the most popular full name.
— *CHINA DAILY*, JUNE 12, 2007

Drivers named Ben are most likely to crash their cars; Ians are the safest.
— *THE GUARDIAN*, JULY 8, 2006

Molly is the most popular name for both dogs and cats in Britain.
— YAHOO NEWS, MAY 28, 2007

There are over sixty people with the first name "Hitler" in Venezuela.

— *THE NEW YORK TIMES*, SEPTEMBER 5, 2007

Fidel Castro's fascination with Alexander the Great led him to name three of his sons Alexis, Alexander, and Alejandro.

— *THE NEW YORKER*, JULY 31, 2006

In mid-2004, "Mohammed" was the most popular name for newborn boys in Amsterdam.

— *THE ATLANTIC*, JUNE 2004

Of almost three thousand public schools in Florida, five are named after George Washington, compared with eleven named after manatees.

— *WHAT'S IN A NAME? THE DECLINE IN THE CIVIC MISSION OF SCHOOL NAMES* BY JAY P. GREENE, BRIAN KISIDA, AND JONATHAN BUTCHER

Nearly 3,500 Chinese children have been named after the Olympics. Most of the children named Aoyun (Mandarin for "Olympics") are males born around 2000, when Beijing was bidding to host the games. Another 4,000 children share names with the Games mascots. —*METRO*, NOVEMBER 5, 2007

Mao Zedong had a hairdresser called Big Beard Wang. —*THE AGE*, AUGUST 26, 2006

"Lula"—the Brazilian president's nickname—means "squid" in Portuguese. —*FORTUNE*, NOVEMBER 1, 2004

Harry S Truman had no middle name. His advisers insisted he insert an initial to gain credibility with voters. —*MONITOR*, FEBRUARY 1, 2008

Ghanaians are often named after the day of the week on which they were born. Kofi Annan was born on a Friday. —CROSS-CULTURAL SOLUTIONS

Marlboro cigarettes take their name from Great Marlborough Street—the location of the Philip Morris factory that first produced them.

—LONDONIST.COM, FEBRUARY 18, 2008

In 1982, a law was passed in Zimbabwe banning jokes about President Canaan Banana's name.

—*THE ECONOMIST*, NOVEMBER 29, 2003

There are around twenty families with the name Obama in the United States, compared with more than 11,000 Clintons and 60,000 Bushes.

—*THE WASHINGTON POST*, NOVEMBER 28, 2008

People named Paul have appeared on fifty-seven number-one singles since the British chart began in 1953; the runner-up name is John, with fifty-four.

—BBC NEWS ONLINE, JULY 25, 2007

Surnames were illegal in Mongolia from the early
1920s until 1997, when they were legally reintro-
duced. But 10,000 people still have only one name.

—TORONTO *GLOBE AND MAIL,* MAY 12, 2004

In California, 30 percent of black female newborns
are given names unique among all newborns in the
state that year.

—SLATE, APRIL 11, 2005

British men with the same last name have a 24 percent chance of sharing a common ancestor. The odds
increase to nearly 50 percent if the surname is rare.

—UNITED PRESS INTERNATIONAL, OCTOBER 9, 2008

In 1377, 35 percent of English men were named
John.

—*THE OBSERVER,* MARCH 14, 2004

There are more people called Chang in China than
there are people in Germany.

—STEPHEN GREEN, CHAIRMAN, HSBC

DO BLONDES REALLY HAVE MORE FUN?
Facts About Hair Color

In the urban West, one out of three women has blond hair; only one in 20 is a blonde by nature. —*ON BLONDES* BY JOANNA PITMAN

\!?\!

On average, redheads require 20 percent more anesthetic than people with different colored hair. —UNIVERSITY OF LOUISVILLE

\!?\!

Red is the rarest shade of hair color in existence. Britain and Ireland have a higher proportion of redheads than any other country.
—*THE GUARDIAN*, JUNE 5, 2007

\!?\!

Sixty-two of the world's 100 richest men are married to brunettes, twenty-two to blondes, sixteen to "raven-haired" women, and none to a redhead. —LYCOS

Holy Cow!

Facts About Religion

Seven of America's nine founding fathers denied the divinity of Jesus.   —*HARPER'S*, JULY 2005

The only major religion not to endorse abstinence from food on special occasions is Sikhism.
                                   —*THE NEW YORKER*, SEPTEMBER 3, 2007

Only 15 percent of Estonians believe in God, making them the least religious nation in the European Union.   —*METRO*, JUNE 6, 2007

Only 31 percent of Christian activists in the United States believe that a person can be both a good Christian and a liberal.

—INSTITUTE FOR FIRST AMENDMENT STUDIES

In the United States, Muslims outnumber Jews.

—ALI MAZRUI, RSA LECTURE

Just 1.4 percent of Iran's population attend Friday prayers.

—OPENDEMOCRACY.NET, FEBRUARY 14, 2006

In the United States, there are more Mormons than Jews under the age of forty-five.

—*PROSPECT*, NOVEMBER 2006

Cambridge University Press removed the date of creation of the world (4004 B.C.) from its edition of the Bible in 1900.

—*AEONS* BY MARTIN GORST

There are 23,000 different Christian denominations worldwide. — *TOWER OF BABEL* BY ROBERT T. PENNOCK

In early 2007, the proportion of French people who described themselves as Catholic was 51 percent, down from 62 percent in just four years.

— *THE INDEPENDENT*, JANUARY 22, 2007

One-third to one-half of America's Christians have changed denominations in their lives.

— *PROSPECT*, JANUARY 2004

When Pope John Paul II was elected in 1978, the Holy See had full ties with 85 states worldwide. When he died, the figure was 174.

— *THE ECONOMIST*, JULY 19, 2007

Only thirty countries do not have a religious or ethnic minority constituting at least 10 percent of the population. —ECONOMIST.COM, JULY 15, 2004

Protestants make up 15 percent of the population of Latin America—up from 3 percent in just ten years. The Catholic proportion has dropped from 80 to 70 percent.

—THE ECONOMIST, OCTOBER 29, 2005

Islam has overtaken Catholicism as the biggest religious denomination in the world. Muslims make up 19.2 percent of the world's population and Catholics 17.4 percent.

—REUTERS, MARCH 30, 2008

John Kerry was only the third Catholic to be nominated for the U.S. presidency, after Al Smith in 1928 and John F. Kennedy in 1960.

—INTERNATIONAL HERALD TRIBUNE, MAY 11, 2004

To cover the £1.25 million cost of his visit to Mexico in 1999, the Pope had twenty-five official sponsors, including Pepsi.

—THE INDEPENDENT, JANUARY 23, 1999

Catholics believe that the soul comes into existence at the exact moment of conception. In Greek Orthodoxy, "ensoulment" happens at twenty-one days, in Islam at forty days, and in Judaism at eighty days.

— *BETWEEN THE MONSTER AND THE SAINT* BY RICHARD HOLLOWAY

Back to Nature

Facts About Our Earth and Its Resources

Every year, the world's deserts produce 1.7 billion tons of dust.

—BBC

Nature reserves and national parks cover 3 percent of the world's surface.

—PANOS MEDIA BRIEFING NO. 25

Canada has over 200,000 kilometers of coastline—almost four times as much as the next country Indonesia, which has around 58,000 kilometers.

—CIA WORLD FACTBOOK

More than 80 percent of the new global oil reserves discovered between 2001 and 2004 were in west Africa. —*LONDON REVIEW OF BOOKS*, JULY 5, 2007

Over 99.9 percent of the land on Earth is not occupied by a person at a given time.

—ASSOCIATED PRESS, FEBRUARY 20, 2008

Oslo is about the same distance from Rome as it is from the northernmost point of the Norwegian landmass. —*PROSPECT* RESEARCH

A tenth of the world's population relies on the river Ganges for water. —BBC WORLD

The Amazon River's course is 3,900 miles, the distance from New York to Rome.

—*INTERNATIONAL HERALD TRIBUNE*, DECEMBER 21, 2000

Only 5 percent of land in the United States is urban-ized.

—MICHAEL CRICHTON, SPEECH GIVEN TO COMMONWEALTH CLUB
IN SAN FRANCISCO, SEPTEMBER 15, 2003,

❓

Nearly half of the carbon dioxide emitted by humans since the beginning of the nineteenth century has been absorbed by the oceans.

— THE NEW YORKER, NOVEMBER 20, 2006

❗

It takes one hundred years for the deep-sea clam to grow to the length of a third of an inch.

— THE BOOK OF USELESS INFORMATION BY KEITH WATERHOUSE
AND RICHARD LITTLEJOHN

❓

An estimated 30 percent of Earth's ice-free land is directly or indirectly involved in livestock pro-duction.

— THE NEW YORK TIMES, JANUARY 27, 2008

❗

Since the formation of the solar system 4.6 billion years ago, the sun has become 25 to 30 percent hotter. —CARL SAGAN

Assuming that only 10 percent of the oil in the tar sands of Alberta, Canada, is recoverable, it still represents the second largest reserve in the world, after Saudi Arabia—more than Kuwait, Norway, and Russia combined. —*THE NEW YORKER*, NOVEMBER 12, 2007

More than 90 percent of the world's rubies come from Burma. —*THE SUNDAY TIMES*, SEPTEMBER 30, 2007

The average ratio between the actual length of a meandering river and its length as the crow flies is pi. —*FERMAT'S ENIGMA* BY SIMON SINGH

Lake Baikal in Russia contains about 20 percent of the world's fresh water. —BBC.CO.UK, JULY 29, 2008

Q

If you could gather every scrap of gold ever mined into one place, you could only build about one-third of the Washington Monument with it. All of the platinum ever mined would easily fit in the average home.

—MONEY.HOWSTUFFWORKS.COM

More Bang for Your Buck!

Facts About the Economy

In 2004, GDP per head in the European Union as a whole was higher than only Arkansas, Montana, West Virginia, and Mississippi among the fifty U.S. states.
— *THE NEW YORK TIMES*, APRIL 17, 2005

Seventy percent of the trade tariffs paid by developing countries are to other developing countries.
—LINNET F. DEILY, FORMER U.S. AMBASSADOR TO THE WTO

With its foreign exchange reserves, China could buy every single publicly quoted African company.
—ECONOMIST.COM, JULY 29, 2007

Of India's 1.1 billion people, only 35 million pay income tax. — *THE NEW YORK TIMES*, JANUARY 17, 2007

Five percent of China's GDP is exported directly to Wal-Mart. — *THE OBSERVER*, DECEMBER 19, 2004

In 2007, total European stock market capitalization exceeded that of the United States for the first time since 1945.

—PAUL KENNEDY, LECTURE AT LONDON SCHOOL OF ECONOMICS, FEBRUARY 6, 2008

In 1820, China and India contributed nearly half of the world's income; by 1950, their share had fallen to less than one-tenth. Today, it is just less than one-fifth. — *BOSTON REVIEW*, JANUARY/FEBRUARY 2008

In 2003, the World Trade Organization's budget was less than a quarter of the World Wide Fund for Nature's. —*FOREIGN POLICY*, JANUARY/FEBRUARY 2003

In 1820, Asia accounted for 56 percent of world output. In 1900, the figure was about 32 percent. Today, it is just over one-third. —*PROSPECT* RESEARCH

Just 6.5 percent of Chinese government revenue comes from income tax. —*THE WALL STREET JOURNAL*, FEBRUARY 11, 2008

The World Bank lent $1 billion less to Africa from July 2006 to April 2007 than in the same period a year earlier. —*THE NEW YORKER*, APRIL 9, 2007

In 1978, China's economy was smaller than Belgium's. —*THE UNDERCOVER ECONOMIST* BY TIM HARFORD

Three times as much money is invested by rich Africans in foreign bank accounts as is sent to the continent as remittances by overseas African workers.
— *PROSPECT*, FEBRUARY 2006

For several years, the annual expansion in China's trade has been larger than India's total annual trade.
— VOXEU.ORG

At the beginning of the eighteenth century, India's GDP was the largest in the world.
— TIMESONLINE.CO.UK, JANUARY 17, 2003

In 1945, the United States was responsible for half of world GDP. The figure is now about 20 percent.
— PAUL KENNEDY, LECTURE AT LONDON SCHOOL OF ECONOMICS, FEBRUARY 6, 2008

China produces less than 4 percent of the world's exports, India less than 1 percent.

— *THE UNDERCOVER ECONOMIST* BY TIM HARFORD

The European Union exports more to Switzerland than to China.   — *THE WALL STREET JOURNAL*, JUNE 12, 2007

On September 29, 2008, the day that the U.S. Congress rejected the Paulson plan and the Dow dropped 7 percent, the only stock in the S&P 500 that rose was Campbell Soup Company.

—ECONOMIST.COM, SEPTEMBER 30, 2008

The Past Is a Foreign Country

Facts About History

During the first year of the Nazi invasion of the Soviet Union, the Red Army issued 800,000 death sentences to its own soldiers.

— *NO SIMPLE VICTORY* BY NORMAN DAVIES

From 1964 to 1968, the U.S. government devoted 4 percent of the federal budget to the Apollo space program. — *THE SUNDAY TIMES MAGAZINE*, OCTOBER 7, 2007

Slavery was legal in Saudi Arabia until the 1960s.

— *PROSPECT*, APRIL 2002

In 1967, 1,353 dependents of Civil War veterans were still receiving government benefits.

—FOREIGN POLICY PASSPORT, NOVEMBER 26, 2007

Q

Until the late 1960s, men with long hair were not allowed to enter Disneyland. —PROSPECT RESEARCH

Q

The earliest recorded reference to bagpipes is on a Hittite slab from Asia Minor, which has been dated to 1000 B.C. —VISITSCOTLAND.COM

Q

Three thousand guillotine executions were carried out in Paris during the Terror; ten thousand were carried out under the Nazis in 1944 and 1945 alone.

—GUILLOTINE: THE TIMBERS OF JUSTICE BY ROBERT FREDERICK OPIE

Q

Until 1972, you had to be a householder to sit on a jury in Britain. —MIND THE GAP BY FERDINAND MOUNT

Q

From 1946 to 1978, South Korea received nearly as much U.S. aid as Africa.

— *THE NEW YORKER,* JULY 25, 2005

❓

The first year in which there was no recorded lynching of a black American was 1952.

— *THE BOSTON GLOBE,* DECEMBER 2, 2007

❗

In 1900, Americans spent nearly twice as much on funerals as on medicine, and less than 2 percent took holidays. — *THE NEW YORK TIMES,* JUNE 10, 2007

❓

In 1910, 20 percent of the world's Swedes lived in the United States. — *THE ECONOMIST,* JUNE 14, 2003

❗

On average, in every year between the middle of the sixteenth century and the end of the seventeenth, Russia expanded its territory by land area equal to the size of the Netherlands.

— *THE NEW YORK REVIEW OF BOOKS,* OCTOBER 7, 2004

A quarter of the estimated 60,000 witches executed in Europe between 1450 and 1750 were men.

—*MALE WITCHES IN EARLY MODERN EUROPE*
BY LARA APPS AND ANDREW GOW

Ⓠ

Up to a third of the Libyan population is estimated to have died during the Italian occupation in the 1930s.

—*THE NEW YORKER*, MAY 8, 2006

Ⓠ

Pakistan's first budget devoted nearly two-thirds of resources to defense.

—*PROSPECT*, DECEMBER 2007

Ⓠ

The following events in German history all took place on November 9: the abdication of the Kaiser and the proclamation of the Republic (1918), the failure of the Munich beer-hall putsch (1923), Kristallnacht (1938), and the fall of the Berlin Wall (1989).

—THE VIRTUAL STOA

Ⓠ

In 1928, the British Parliament passed the Easter Act, which fixed Easter Sunday as the first Sunday after the second Saturday in April. It has never been implemented.

—BBC.CO.UK

🄰

In the Second World War, every Italian soldier in North Africa carried his own personal espresso machine.

—*ESSENTIAL MILITARIA* BY NICHOLAS HOBBES

🄰

More slave laborers died building the V-2 rocket than were ever killed by it.

—*THE SHOCK OF THE NEW* BY DAVID EDGERTON

🄰

In 1969, an American urologist bought Napoleon's mummified penis at auction.

—*THE NEW YORK TIMES*, MAY 13, 2007

🄰

On the night before the Queen's coronation in 1953, 30,000 people slept in the Mall.

—MUSEUM OF LONDON

🄰

Five hundred people were trampled to death in
Moscow on the day of Stalin's funeral in 1953.

— RUSSIA: A HISTORY, EDITED BY GREGORY FREEZE

Between Black Thursday and the end of 1929, only
four of the one hundred suicides and suicide attempts reported in *The New York Times* were jumps
from buildings linked to the stock market crash.

—SLATE, SEPTEMBER 22, 2008

Hail to the Chief

Facts About Politics and Politicians

On the day after George W. Bush's reelection in 2004, Immigration Canada's website received a record 179,000 hits, with 64 percent originating in the U.S.

—BBC.CO.UK

In 2004, the Texas Democratic party had no full-time staff.

—*THE NEW REPUBLIC*, APRIL 13, 2006

In the U.S., abortions fell by 17 percent throughout the 1990s, reaching a twenty-four-year low when George W. Bush took office in 2001. Then they started to rise again.

—SOJOMAIL

In the twentieth century, democratic government turned into authoritarian rule around the world more than seventy times.

— *FOREIGN AFFAIRS*, MAY/JUNE 1999

The most widely known fact about George H. W. Bush in the 1992 presidential election was that he hated broccoli. Eighty-six percent of likely voters knew that the Bushes' dog was called Millie; only 15 percent knew that Bush and Clinton both favored the death penalty. — *THE NEW YORKER*, AUGUST 30, 2004

In 2005, the Texas House of Representatives passed the "booty bill," prohibiting "overly sexually sugges-tive" performances by cheerleaders.

— *THE ECONOMIST*, SEPTEMBER 2, 2006

Without the black vote, the Democrats would have won the U.S. presidency only once, in 1964.

— *THE GUARDIAN*, SEPTEMBER 18, 2006

France has 36,782 mayors. Among them are the
elected mayors of five villages that ceased to exist
ninety-two years ago.

— *THE INDEPENDENT,* FEBRUARY 29, 2008

In India, unlike most advanced democracies, elec-
toral participation is positively correlated with
poverty.

— *MAXIMUM CITY* BY SUKETU MEHTA

The Clintons sent 400,000 Christmas cards in 2000.
In their first year in office, Laura and George W.
Bush sent 875,000. In 2002, they sent one million,
in 2003 1.3 million, and in 2004, two million.

— *INTERNATIONAL HERALD TRIBUNE,* DECEMBER 13, 2004

Jon Corzine spent more money winning his New
Jersey Senate seat in 2000 than the total spent by
every political party in the British general election
of 2001.

— *THE NEW YORK REVIEW OF BOOKS,* MAY 15, 2003

In the 2000 U.S. presidential election, the five rich-
est states all voted for Al Gore, while George W.
Bush took the fourteen poorest states (apart from
New Mexico).   *—FINANCIAL TIMES*, JULY 24, 2004

Mitch Daniels, George W. Bush's first budget direc-
tor, tried (and failed) to get the Office of Manage-
ment and Budget to use "You Can't Always Get What
You Want" by the Rolling Stones as its hold music.
                        —THE ECONOMIST, NOVEMBER 4, 2006

In the United States, more than one million elections
are held in every four-year period.
            —BRING HOME THE REVOLUTION BY JONATHAN FREEDLAND

Six future U.S. presidents were born between 1911
and 1924. None were born between 1925 and 1946,
although John McCain was born in 1936.
                            —PROSPECT RESEARCH

Thirty-five percent of Turks say they believe their country is "governed according to the will of the people," more than in Britain (30 percent), France (26), or Germany (18).

—THE VOICE OF THE PEOPLE SURVEY 2006

In the United States, 45 percent of Republicans say they are happy, compared to 29 percent of Democrats.   —PEW RESEARCH CENTER FOR THE PEOPLE & THE PRESS

In the eight years after the end of the Cold War, 504 resolutions were put before the U.N. Security Council. During the previous forty-five years, there were 659.

—ALAN MUNRO, FORMER UK AMBASSADOR TO SAUDI ARABIA

Fifty-six percent of the donations from professional athletes and executives to the 2008 presidential campaigns went to John McCain, and 44 percent to Barack Obama.

—ESPN

Nine out of ten Chinese citizens say they approve of the way things are going in their country.

— *THE NEW YORKER*, JULY 28, 2008

Barack Obama is left-handed, as were presidents Gerald Ford, Ronald Reagan, George H.W. Bush, and Bill Clinton; presidential candidates Al Gore, Bob Dole, John Edwards, Bill Bradley, Ross Perot and John McCain; and Michael Bloomberg, the mayor of New York.

— *NEW YORK SUN*, JUNE 23, 2008.

Roughly 10 percent of all U.S. presidents ever elected have been assassinated (four out of forty-three), which is roughly as high an occupational death rate as for street drug dealers.

— CROOKED TIMBER, DECEMBER 23, 2008

The political leadership of Hamas is probably the most highly educated in the world, boasting more than five hundred PhDs in its ranks.

— *THE TIMES*, DECEMBER 31, 2008

War of the Worlds

Facts About Conflict

More explosive power was dropped on Serbia in 1999 than during the entire Vietnam war.

—ROBERT FOX

In 2002, there were 199 terrorist incidents recorded worldwide—the lowest total since 1969.

—U.S. STATE DEPARTMENT

The secular Tamil Tigers in Sri Lanka have been responsible for more suicide bombings than any other terrorist organization in the world—up to two-thirds of the total committed.

—PBS

In the Second World War, 1.8 percent of Americans serving in the armed forces were killed in action. In Vietnam that figure dropped to 0.6 percent, and in the Gulf War to just 0.005 percent.

—PROSPECT, APRIL 2003

Q

Since 1975, there have been nearly 150 terrorist attacks against Americans or American interests in Greece. —FOREIGN POLICY PASSPORT, NOVEMBER 20, 2007

Q

A study of the 101 known suicide bombers in Iraq from March 2003 to February 2006 found that only seven were from Iraq. Eight were from Italy.

—THE NEW REPUBLIC, JANUARY 22, 2007

Q

In 2004, only three European countries had laws against "apology" for or "glorification" of terrorism. By November 2006, thirty-six countries had committed to criminalizing the "provocation" of terrorism.

—HUMAN RIGHTS WATCH WORLD REPORT 2007

Q

China contributes more than twice as many troops to U.N. peacekeeping missions as any other member of the Security Council. — *FOREIGN POLICY*, MAY 9, 2006

In both Vietnam and the Falklands wars, more troops committed suicide after the conflict than were killed during it. — *PROSPECT* RESEARCH

For every insurgent killed in Iraq, 250,000 bullets have been fired.

— *THE WASHINGTON POST*, NOVEMBER 18, 2007

Britain and France, followed by the United States and Russia/USSR, have fought the most international wars since 1946. — HUMAN SECURITY REPORT 2005

Around 2.4 percent of the world's population was killed in the Second World War and 0.5 percent in the first, compared with 0.2 percent in the Napoleonic Wars. — *THE CASH NEXUS* BY NIALL FERGUSON

During the 1864–70 López war between Paraguay and the triple alliance (Argentina, Brazil, and Peru), Paraguay's population fell from 1.3 million to 221,000.   —*ESSENTIAL MILITARIA* BY NICHOLAS HOBBES

When Hitler invaded the Soviet Union, his army used more horses per soldier than Napoleon's invading army had done over a hundred years earlier.
                                          —*PROSPECT,* APRIL 2002

Inheritance tax was invented by the emperor Augustus to raise funds for soldiers' pensions.
                          —*BBC NEWS MAGAZINE,* OCTOBER 10, 2007

The Thirty Years' War in the early seventeenth century led to the death of 30 percent of the population of Germany.   —*THE ATLANTIC,* MARCH 2008

A third of the population of Belarus died in the Second World War.   —*THE ECONOMIST,* OCTOBER 16, 2004

❓

As a percentage of population, Australia sustained more losses in the First World War than any other nation.

—EVERYTHING YOU DIDN'T NEED TO KNOW ABOUT AUSTRALIA BY ADAM WARD

6,706,993,152 and Counting

Facts About the World's Population

In January 2007, the title "world's oldest person" changed hands three times. —*HARPER'S*, APRIL 2007

Since 1980, the population of the "greater Middle East" (thirty mainly Muslim countries from Morocco in the west to Bangladesh in the east) has nearly doubled, from 350 million to 600 million, while its share of the world exports has fallen from 13.5 percent to 4 percent. —PROGRESSIVE POLICY INSTITUTE

Ireland has a million fewer inhabitants than in the 1850s. —*PROSPECT*, MAY 2008

In 2005, there were over 25,000 centenarians in Japan—twice as many as five years earlier. By 2050, the country expects to have more than one million people over the age of one hundred.

—THE ASSOCIATED PRESS, SEPTEMBER 13, 2005

By 2050, Ukraine's population is expected to fall 43 percent from its 2004 level.

— THE ECONOMIST, JANUARY 7, 2005

Since 1991, 1.5 million people have emigrated from the old East Germany—over two-thirds of them women.

—BERLIN INSTITUTE FOR POPULATION AND DEVELOPMENT

The foreign-born population of the United States peaked around 1890, at 15 percent. It is currently around 10 percent. —ECONOMIST.COM, MAY 23, 2007

The U.S. population reached 100 million in 1915, 200 million in 1967, and 300 million in 2006.

— *THE NEW YORK TIMES*, JANUARY 13, 2006

Moscow has a Muslim population of about 2.5 million—the largest of any European city. Since 1989, Russia's Muslim population has increased by 40 percent, to about 25 million.

— *SAN FRANCISCO CHRONICLE*, NOVEMBER 19, 2006

In China in 1996, there were 121 boys between the ages of one and four for every 100 girls in the same age range.

— *THE CHRONICLE OF HIGHER EDUCATION*, APRIL 30, 2004

Forty-seven percent of children under five in India are malnourished—more than in sub-Saharan Africa.

— *THE ECONOMIST*, JANUARY 6, 2007

Fifty percent of the entire wealth of Russia is in the hands of just five hundred people.

—SKY

The number of Americans who say they consider themselves to be among the "have-nots" has risen from 17 to 34 percent since 1988.

—*HARPER'S*, JANUARY 2008

Iran's population is only 51 percent Persian.

—*LOS ANGELES TIMES*, OCTOBER 25, 2006

Nineteen percent of the Canadian population are immigrants.

—*FOREIGN POLICY*, FEBRUARY 2008

Seventy-one percent of Russians do not see themselves as European.

—*MOSCOW TIMES*, MARCH 1, 2007

The percentage of Nigerians living on less than a dollar a day has risen from 32 percent in 1985 to 71 percent today.

—*HARPER'S*, FEBRUARY 2007

Ninety-seven percent of young Irish people have vis-
ited the United Kingdom.

—*THROUGH IRISH EYES,* BRITISH COUNCIL

There are 123,598,000 Muslims living in India—
only slightly fewer than the 140,277,000 that live in
Pakistan. —CIA WORLD FACTBOOK

There are more Arabs in Brazil than in the Palestinian territories.

—*THE WASHINGTON POST,* NOVEMBER 19, 2007

Brazil has more people of African descent than any
country outside Africa. —BBC

In the last two hundred years, France has taken in
more immigrants than any other European country.

—BLOOMBERG, FEBRUARY 26, 2008

Mississippi is the fattest state, with 32.6 percent of the population classified as obese in 2007. The leanest state is Colorado, at 19.3 percent.

—CALORIELAB.COM

BAD HABITS

Facts to Make You Change Your Ways

In the United States, tobacco kills nearly half
a million people annually; more than HIV, alcohol, illegal drugs, suicide, and homicide
combined.

—TIMES LITERARY SUPPLEMENT, SEPTEMBER 28, 2007

!?!

Women who receive implants for breast en-
hancement are three times more likely to
commit suicide than other women.

—LOS ANGELES TIMES, AUGUST 8, 2007

!?!

The average Greek smokes three thousand
cigarettes a year.

—ECONOMIST.COM, MAY 15, 2007

!?!

Children who bathe every day and wash
their hands more than five times a day are
25 percent more likely to have asthma than
those who don't.

—JEAN GOLDING, UNIVERSITY OF BRISTOL

!?!

Seventy percent of mental health inpatients are smokers, compared to 26 percent of the general population.　　　—MENTAL HEALTH TODAY

!?!

Smoking is responsible for 25 percent of all male deaths in the developed world.
　　　　　　　　　　　　—WORLD HEALTH ORGANIZATION

Get Outta Here!

Facts to Surprise and Stun Your Friends

NASA has never had a space shuttle in the air during the transition from December 31 to January 1. It is not confident about the onboard software coping with the switch.

—*LONDON REVIEW OF BOOKS*, MARCH 6, 2008

The Eiffel Tower is six inches taller in summer than in winter.

—MICHELIN *GREEN GUIDE*

If all the Lego pieces in the world were divided up evenly, we would get thirty each.

—*DAD STUFF* BY STEVE CAPLIN AND SIMON ROSE

A billion seconds ago, it was 1977. A billion minutes ago, Jesus had only recently died. A billion hours ago, our ancestors were living in the Stone Age.

—SNOPES.COM

The 6.5 billion people alive today make up about 6 percent of the number of people who have ever been born.

—*SCIENTIFIC AMERICAN*, MARCH 1, 2007

There are more atoms in a glass of water than glasses of water in all the oceans in the world.

—*SCIENCE YOU CAN'T SEE: THE ATOM*, BBC4

Most telephones have dial tones in the key of F.

—*THE BOOK OF USELESS INFORMATION* BY KEITH WATERHOUSE AND RICHARD LITTLEJOHN.

A penny dropped from the top of the Empire State Building would do no more than sting a pedestrian at ground level.

—LIVESCIENCE.COM

❶

One ton of computer scrap contains more gold than seventeen tons of gold ore.

— *FOREIGN POLICY*, MAY/JUNE 2007

❓

Over 90 percent of people who attempted to jump off the Golden Gate Bridge but were stopped are either still alive or died of natural causes.

—RICHARD SEIDEN, "WHERE ARE THEY NOW? A FOLLOW-UP STUDY OF SUICIDE ATTEMPTERS FROM THE GOLDEN GATE BRIDGE"

❶

In 1976, Queen Elizabeth II became the first head of state to send an email message.

— *SEND* BY DAVID SHIPLEY AND WILL SCHWALBE

❓

Eleven of the twelve men to have walked on the moon were in the Boy Scouts.

—BOY SCOUTS OF AMERICA NATIONAL COUNCIL

❗

Forty percent of bottled water sold, by volume, is tap water.
—ECONOMIST.COM, JULY 31, 2007

❓

At least 50,000 people have bought testicular implants for their pets.
—DISCOVER YOUR INNER ECONOMIST BY TYLER COWEN

❗

The "close doors" button doesn't work in most elevators.
—THE NEW YORKER, APRIL 21, 2008

❓

The metal value of some pennies exceeds their face value. A penny minted before 1982 is 95 percent copper. At recent prices, this is worth about two and a half cents.
—THE NEW YORKER, MARCH 31, 2008

❗

American Airlines once saved $40,000 by removing a single olive from each salad served in first class.
—THE BUSINESS, MAY 11–12, 2001

In Britain, trousers cause twice as many accidents as chainsaws.

—BRITISH COUNCIL

Each successive monarch faces in a different direction on British coins.

—BBC.CO.UK

The money transfer company Western Union has as many outlets worldwide as McDonald's, Starbucks, Burger King, and Wal-Mart combined.

— THE NEW YORK TIMES, NOVEMBER 22, 2007

The removal of the annual half-ton of droppings from Nelson's column in Trafalgar Square costs London about 35,000 pounds per year.

— MERDE BY RALPH A. LEWIN

Air weighs roughly one kilogram per cubic meter. Large rooms contain several tons of air.

— AN OCEAN OF AIR: A NATURAL HISTORY OF THE
ATMOSPHERE BY GABRIELLE WALKER

The price of lead rose sevenfold between 2002 and 2008. Some English churches have had their roofs stripped of lead by thieves hoping to sell it.

— *THE NEW YORK TIMES,* APRIL 8, 2008

The average woman today has 450 periods over her lifetime, compared with an estimated 160 in her ancestor's.

— *PROSPECT,* SEPTEMBER 2003

As of early 2005, more houses in China had a DVD player than running hot and cold water.

— *THE GUARDIAN,* JANUARY 4, 2005

Since 2002, more than $676 million worth of art has been stolen from European museums.

— *FOREIGN POLICY* PASSPORT, FEBRUARY 11, 2008

In Britain, flowerpots are responsible for 5,300 accidents a year, making them the second most dangerous piece of garden equipment, after lawnmowers.

— *THE GUARDIAN*, MAY 3, 2004

Cuba will lift its ban on toasters in 2010.

— *THE NEW YORK TIMES*, MARCH 14, 2008

As of early 2008, the Simon Wiesenthal Center was still hunting 488 suspected living Nazis.

— *HARPER'S*, JANUARY 2008

No private individual currently owns a certified Vermeer painting.

— *DISCOVER YOUR INNER ECONOMIST* BY TYLER COWEN

Roughly 1 percent of the static a detuned television receives derives from the Big Bang.

— *A SHORT HISTORY OF NEARLY EVERYTHING* BY BILL BRYSON

Ⓠ

The U.S. government directly owns nearly 30 percent of the total territory of the United States. It
owns 84.5 percent of Nevada, but only 0.4 percent of
Rhode Island and Connecticut.

—U.S. GENERAL SERVICES ADMINISTRATION

ABOUT THE AUTHOR

TOM NUTTALL compiled the "In Fact" column, on which this book is based, for *Prospect,* a British magazine of politics and culture, between 2002 and 2008. He lives in London.